T0156748

A Walk On The Other Side

A Young woman's Near Death Experiences that prove the continuity of Life after Death

Charmaine Mary Nona Maeer

authorHOUSE®

AuthorHouse™
1663 Liberty Drive
Bloomington, IN 47403
www.authorhouse.com
Phone: 1-800-839-8640

First published by AuthorHouse   5/25/2011

ISBN: 978-1-4567-8273-3 (sc)
ISBN: 978-1-4567-8275-7 (e)

Printed in the United States of America

Any people depicted in stock imagery provided by Thinkstock are models, and such images are being used for illustrative purposes only. Certain stock imagery © Thinkstock.

This book is printed on acid-free paper.

Dedication

I Dedicate this book to all my family and friends in the Spirit World who have given me the tools to write this book.

Chapter One:
Why Take the Journey?

I have had many near-death experiences in my life, and to this day I can count four which changed my life forever. I have suffered many traumas from a young age, and these traumas changed something within me that has altered the way I view life here on Earth and after death. I feel like I have walked in my 'spirit shoes' many times, and on all these journeys I was shown and told many things about life here on Earth and in Spirit.

I was born a natural medium and healer, following in the footsteps of my mother and my grandmother, who were both well-known and respected mediums. Both of them travelled far and wide in England to different Spiritualist churches to show their gifts to people, and to demonstrate that there was a life after death, and to prove this to those who longed to make contact with their loved ones who had passed on before them.

My mother and grandmother were also asked on a number of occasions by the local police in their area to help with solving murder cases and crimes that the police themselves found hard to solve. My mother would go with my gran to the police headquarters and sit with the main police officers on the case and speak with spirits to see what information they could pass on from the Spirit World that would be of help to the case. I do know that one of the cases involved the murder of a young child, and both my mum and gran helped solve this case and were in the local newspapers. There were also cases from Scotland and Ireland where there was a number of murders – some like Jack the Ripper in that no one could solve the case – and the officers would travel down to see my mum and gran and ask for their help from Spirit to gain some information to unravel the mystery behind the case. There was also the case of the Great Train Robbery of August 1963, and my mum and gran gave the police information from Spirit in solving this case and answering the many questions behind it. The Great Train Robbery is the name given to a £2.6 million train robbery committed on August 8 1963 at the Bridego railway bridge in Ledburn near Mentmore in Buckinghamshire, England. The bulk of the stolen money was never recovered. This was probably the largest robbery in terms of the amount stolen in British history.

The Glasgow-to-London Euston travelling post office train was stopped by a red signal light at Sears crossing. Unknown to the driver, the signal had been tampered with; a glove was placed over the green light and a six volt battery temporarily powered the red one. The locomotive fireman, Dave Parr, went to call the signalman, only to find the telephone cable had been cut. Upon returning to the train, he was thrown down the railway embankment beside the track. It is said that one robber had spent months befriending railway staff and familiarising himself with the layout of the railway, so that all would go to plan. The fifteen members of the railway gang included Bruce Reynolds and Ronnie Biggs. Although no guns were used, the train driver was hit on the head with a metal bar. He lived, but his life was always full of trauma headaches because of this.

My mum and gran gave the police information they had received from the Spirit World, and the police went to Leatherslade farm near Oakley, Buckinghamshire five days after the robbery and after receiving this information from my mum and gran. There they found fingerprints of the robbers, including those on the Monopoly board game that had been used after the robbery, with the gang members playing with real money.

Also, after these cases, my mum and gran would do what is called a 'spirit rescue' to help the poor souls that were victims in the crimes move on to the Spirit World after their trauma. They would always be offered a reward, but they both said it should go to charity, even though they were not very well off and would have needed the money. My mother and gran were such caring loveable people, and everyone who needed help would come to them and chat with them about their problems. It was as though everyone wanted them to be their friend because of the warmth and care which they gave to people.

My grandmother was a chef in the Army and Royal Air Force who met and later married an officer in the Army. The story behind their meeting is very funny and sums up my gran's character well. One night my gran had finished her work in the army kitchen and was ready to go home when a man appeared and announced that he would like a bacon sandwich. Gran told him firmly that she wouldn't do this, but he ignored her reply and said that one of his men would collect it once it was ready! My gran was a lady of fire (much like me), and she decided to teach him a lesson he would not forget. She rummaged in the bins until she found some old bacon rinds and made these into a nice-looking sandwich! When his man came to collect the sandwich, my gran smiled as she told him to enjoy it. Well, I guess when he got the sandwich he wasn't too pleased. He was taken aback, but he must have seen a good woman in this and found it very amusing, and he fell in love with this lady of character. The next day he went to see her and smiled and asked her to go out with him. At first she sternly refused, but after a while she must have taken him up on the offer. After a time they married, and so my gran would travel with him around the country with their children. Wherever the army sent him, she would have to go and make a home with the other women and their children.

During this time, my gran didn't dare to say that she could see and hear Spirits, because her husband and his family were strict Catholics, and she had to hide the fact that she was able to sense all these things. But she didn't hide it completely, because all the women and children at the various places she lived with her husband would come to her for advice on their illnesses and their children's mysterious health problems. My gran would look at each person, lay her hands over them, and tell them what she saw in them and how best to treat it. This seemed normal amongst the women, and after a while word spread, and more would come and seek her advice. I guess that in some ways she was the village medicine woman, and she held secrets about how to deal with illness that were not even known by the doctors in those days.

After my gran experienced a tragedy in her own life, she decided to tell people more about her gifts. It was while she was at one of the many army locations with her husband that she was hit by the death of her first son, John, aged five years old. He was out playing, when he ran under a car belonging to one of the army officers. He had severe brain injury, and after nursing him for a month, my gran lost him to Spirit. My gran was very close to this little boy, and she was so broken by this tragedy that she felt she couldn't go on. It was while she was at this lowest point in her life that one night she saw John appear to her by the bed and utter the words, 'I am okay, Mummy, and I love you.' She knew then that her baby boy was safe and well, and she knew that there was truly a life after death and that she must go on with her life until the time came for her to join him.

From that time, she started to talk to people about her gifts and let them know that there was a better life after death for all of us. She was met with some strange looks at this revelation, but others wanted to know more and came to question her. Her husband didn't care much what she was saying, and I guess he just put it down to 'women's talk', but from that day she knew that she had to spread the word of the Spirit World.

My mum would often take me as a child to the Spiritualist churches where she did her work, and I always remember her standing on the platform in the churches and giving people messages of joy from the World of Spirit. I would see people almost jump out of their seats and gasp as they were given information that only they could know. I felt so proud that this was my mum doing this, and I wanted to be like her when I grew up.

From when I was very young, I had a psychic ability to see, hear, and sense Spirit on many occasions. It was not unusual for me at even the age of three to be telling my mum what I could see and what the 'spirit people' (as I called them) were saying to me. I would turn around to my mum or gran and say that I had seen a lady holding out her hands to me, and I would describe this lady really well and see the look on my gran's face as she cried and told me that I was describing her mother. There was no way I could have known what she looked like, because she had died when my gran was just a little girl herself.

I never saw anything strange about this ability, for it seemed so natural to me that I thought that all children could see these other people. So I did not know that there was anything different about me. I guess also that because my family were all spiritually minded, they never appeared shocked about my accounts of what I had seen. In our family it was quite normal to speak of these things.

My sister also was very psychic and would speak of Spirit. On many occasions she saw our late grandfather, especially if she was ill, and she said he would comfort her and help her back to sleep. She didn't seem as keen as I was to share all of what she saw, but she was happy to grow up talking about the Spirit World, as all my family did.

I also felt that I was a natural healer, as I would often feel a warmth in my hands when I was around people who were sick. Often I would be drawn to a family member, and I would rest my tiny hand on their head and tell them that I could make them well. Once, when I was a six-year-old child out with my mum, I had a strange urge to approach a lady in the street to touch her and give her this feeling from my hands. To my mum's amazement, I told the lady, 'I can heal you.' Mum quickly pulled me back and apologised to the lady. However, the lady began to cry and said that her doctor had just told her that she had cancer. She told my mum that she was feeling very lonely and scared, and the small kindness I had shown her would remain with her. She said that she had just been praying for an answer from God to tell her he was with her, and she felt I had just given it to her.

After that event, my healing work as a child was encouraged, and my mum taught me that I must ask to help people before I jumped in, just in case they didn't feel the same way as I did. Well, as a child I didn't know what she meant, and I found it too exciting to share this care and warmth with people. I loved the feelings I got, and I would question my gran often all about the world and ask her to explain why I had this warmth in my hands. She was so patient and loving. She would share with me all her knowledge and experiences, and I would sit on her lap and listen eagerly for more.

I had many pets as a child, and when they became old and sick and tired. I would always offer them the healing I had in my hands, and I would spend hours touching them and trying my best to make them well, or at least comfortable. I loved doing this. It seemed so natural and normal to me to help animals and people.

I guess by today's standards, I would have been called a 'nutter' as a child, but these experiences were real to me, and I was very lucky to have a family who didn't condemn them. At primary school, I would often speak to the children about the feelings I had in my hands, and they wouldn't laugh at me but would ask me to 'do the healing' on them. I think that they were very amused at my 'trick' as they called it, and it gave me the chance to practice it more.

I was also born with an unusual birthmark which rested on both my shoulders. The marks looked as if someone had pressed their thumbs deep into my shoulders and had left a mark from this. My gran would say that they were the nail marks of Christ, which meant I would suffer in life but because of this would become a great healer. Just as a child does, I would laugh at her and give her a grin – my childlike way of saying I didn't have a clue what she was on about. I still have these birthmarks today although the grin has now faded because I now know what she told me has come true. In my lifetime I have suffered a lot, but I did become a healer.

I did live a normal life as a child, and I don't want people thinking that my family had some sort of 'religious mania'. That was far from true. My family believed that we are all unique and that no religion or faith should run our lives. I am very proud of the fact I was born to a spiritual family, and I found that this was just the start of my journey into the Spirit World.

Chapter Two:
The Start of a Long Journey

The first time I had a glimpse into the Spirit World it was just that, 'a glimpse'. It happened while I was starting my career in the British Army. I had joined the army wanting to help people as a medic and save lives and at the same time proudly serve my country. I had started my first day in basic army training, and what was to happen to me there was something that I could never have imagined. I was picked out for no reason and was told that I had been chosen to be the 'army prostitute'. I was then told that I would not be training with the other young men and women, but that I would be held in a room where I would carry out my 'special work'. After I had been beaten badly, I was thrown in a cell and left on my own, despite being dehydrated and in a desperate state.

I was held in a room which I started to call my 'cell' and was kept prisoner. Soldiers would come often to beat me and abuse me and tell me that I was only there for their use. I was in their evil hands for ten days, being abused and raped and beaten at every chance they had. Little did I ever know that the abuse and pain that they put me through would give me my first glimpse into the World of Spirit.

On one occasion I was near death's door, and there was no going back. I was very much alone, and there was no one there – only me. The feeling of loneliness was so great that I didn't care to ever think in my short life I could feel this way. The room I was in was dark and cold, and I could hear my own heart beating. My hearing seemed more acute because I could pick up and understand the people outside the room speaking about me in hushed tones. My hearing picked up everything they were saying and more.

I lay there feeling sure that this was the end of my life and that I was about to die. Images of my loved ones floated into my mind, and I missed them like crazy. My mother came into my mind often, and I wished so badly to be with her. I could hear her voice, and it was as though echoes from the past were running around my mind.

The physical pain then stopped, and I felt like it was just my mind that was functioning. I was feeling sad and lonely, so I guess that my mental state was still very much aware. I could still hear my heart beating, and so I focused on it. It seemed the right thing to do – to listen to the final hours of my heart pounding away. People say that the heart is one of the greatest organs of the human body, and so it was that this great organ wasn't giving in without a fight,

It was then I felt that my mind didn't care anymore and that it too was having its final moments. My thoughts turned from my existence as a human being, and it was as though I was just an energy, leaving my physical state behind. I felt like my eyes could see a thousand times greater and I could hear into a thousand rooms that were closed to me. I felt no pain. The only feeling I had was that of a pure love that felt so great I could move with it. This energy felt as if a light bulb had been turned on, and it seemed to grow with every beat of my heart.

Even though my end seemed so dark and lonely, in contrast the energy had warmth as it contained a great love and harmony. That word 'energy' describes how I felt – an 'energy'. I had left the solid matter of a human, moved on from my body without even being aware, and I was the true feeling that resides in all of us all our lives. I was the energy of love and care, and the only way to put it into words is to say that I want you to imagine how it feels when you love someone so dear to you. It may be a mother or a child or a lover. Imagine how you feel when you think of them, and imagine how your heart jumps when they come to mind. If you are like the average human, you will feel love that is so great it makes you happy and it makes you smile. You feel like you could move a mountain for that person, and you feel that the only thing that matters is their love.

Well, that is the feeling I got in my state of Spirit. It was a great feeling of love, and it was just as though I was that feeling and nothing else. I felt as though this energy could move, and it was as if I didn't care if I had a physical body anymore. I was free from pain and hurt, and I knew that I was now on my spirit journey. I knew I was not in a body anymore, and the only feeling I had was that of thought. It was as if my deepest feelings inside of me were expressing the very core of my identity, the very essence of what now was me. There was no physical feeling, only a feeling of energy, and the way that I can describe what it was like is for you to imagine that you are in a deep daydream, in a place that feels real to you because you are in a different state of mind. You are in the daydream, but your physical body is not there. This is how the experience felt, but it was no daydream, for it was very much real, and I had no control over it.

You hear many people say that when they had a near-death experience, they felt they had left their body and were looking down on themselves. Well, that for me wasn't entirely true, but I did have a glimpse of my body, and it was as though I had left my 'shell' behind and it didn't matter anymore. I saw myself as just that – a shell I didn't even want to take that physical body with me. I just knew that the body was no more than my soul's car to drive around in. The real me had stepped outside of that car and was free as a bird in flight. I saw a cord that was running from my stomach to the roof of the room I was in. It was a transparent cord and a few inches thick. It was like the cord that we have at birth that attaches us to our mothers and that brings us into this world. I had heard many times from my mum that when someone is near death, this cord can be seen by mediums or certain people. It is the cord that attaches our soul to the Earth, and so I guess this was the cord I was seeing. However, this cord wasn't for a person I was watching make their passing to the Spirit World, but rather, this was for myself. When I knew I had left my body, I had a jerking feeling just like the one you sometimes get when you are half asleep and you jump in the bed. Well, that was the feeling I got when I knew I was outside of my body. It was quick, and with the jerking feeling I felt I had stepped outside of the physical world and was looking to move on with my true self.

I wasn't scared, because the only feeling in my spiritual being was one of love, and that energy then started me thinking of the love I had on Earth. I felt that the only thing that I seemed to want was to follow a link of love and care. By this I mean that I wanted to hold onto the love that I had felt on the Earth, and it was the only part of me that seemed to matter. I wanted to be with my loved ones on Earth, and I wanted to hear them and feel them and speak with them.

Suddenly, with that feeling, I was at home and I could see my mother sitting on her favourite chair and talking about me. She was wondering how I was getting on, and she was talking about when I had been a child and my dreams of the future. I felt my energy go over to her, and I tried to put that energy of love into her. I wanted so badly to tell her with my voice that I was here and with her! I felt that the more I wanted this, the more the feeling of love grew and the more I seemed to grow as an energy. I wanted to feel her, but I knew I had no hands, and so I willed that feeling and I heard her say with a gasp, 'Something's wrong with Charmaine.' I was so overjoyed with her response that I tried it again, and I tried to touch her, but touch her not with hands but with love. Again she jumped and said she felt a cold breeze. I saw her every thought, and it felt like I could see her soul as well. I saw her every move, and I wanted to tell her that I was okay. I wanted to hold her hand, and the only way I could do that was to think of how much I loved this person and how badly I wanted to feel her. Again it was as though I had touched her, and again she jumped and moved from the chair. I felt the energy of love grow and grow, and I felt so much more alive with this new energy, the real energy of the soul that was now me and my true form. I felt like the energy of Spirit I was now continued to grow as the love and care I felt also grew. It was like a television being plugged into an electric socket and starting to transmit pictures for the first time.

My energy was then taken to my favourite stables, and I was standing near my favourite horse. I could smell the aroma of the muck, and I wanted to touch my dear friend. The horse was a dark bay horse called Perry. I felt that I had to think hard of how she used to feel in order for my energy to touch her. I thought of the times I had ridden her and how she felt and how she made me feel, and with that it was as if I was on her back. I tried to imagine the love I had for horse riding, and with that I could feel that same love and care I had for my mum happen for this friend the horse. I saw with my spirit eyes her ears go up, and she jumped. She didn't seem too bothered that I was a spirit energy, only slightly taken off her guard because I had appeared so quickly. She seemed relaxed and carried on eating in her stable. She watched me, and she seemed to know I was there. People say that animals can see Spirit, and this seemed very true, for she seemed to watch me in just the same way she had watched me when I was in my physical form. I felt my energy grow more, and again I felt I had made a connection with the horse and the things about riding that I had loved so dearly. This connection and feeling seemed to make me feel much more comfortable in my Spirit form. It was as if I was finding my feet and finding that this was the real me and that I no longer belonged in a physical body. I knew I didn't need a voice anymore or a word to describe the feelings I had. These didn't matter anymore; all that seemed to matter was this great energy and the feeling that was contained within it.

It was then that I saw a beautiful light coming towards me, a light that seemed so full of love that I wanted to move towards it. The light was like a summer glow, and it was like a beacon of love wanting me to approach it. I felt my energy go with it, and I heard a familiar voice reach out to me. It was that of my grandmother, who had been a medium and who was now in the Spirit World. I heard this light talk to me with my gran's voice, and yet I couldn't accept it was she. I recognised her voice, but the form was not one that I was used to. She then told me to think of her when she was alive, and I used my energy as I had when I wanted to touch my mother and the horse, and I remembered my grandmother as she had been when she was alive.

I thought back to when I was a child sitting on my gran's knee listening to her stories and feeling close to my darling gran, whom I had loved like another mother. With that, my dear darling gran appeared, and she came to me with open arms. I felt such a warmth – similar to that of the glow of the sun touching your skin. It was as though the energy I was grew more with the energy of my dear gran so near. She held me close, and our energy seemed to become one. I felt like we were able to touch each other as we had done on Earth, and I felt the same physical contact that we feel when we are on Earth. I felt cared for and loved and secure. She told me that she adored me, and she said that I was to leave now and go back to 'Mother Earth', as she put it.

I wanted to remain free, and this energy felt more real to me than my body. I asked her if I could go with her, but she replied that the Universe wasn't ready to give up one of its stars just now. She said the words I will never forget, 'Charmaine, love that will not let you go'. These were words that my gran had often said when I was young. She would say them when she wanted to tell people how much God loved them. The love in her words made me realise that I was to go back and that this wasn't my right time. I wanted to remain with this energy of love and with my gran who was like a mother to me, but I also had a deep feeling that this wasn't my time to stay in this form and that I must return to the Earth and to my body. I have no idea why I felt this way, for I didn't have any desire to go back to pain and to being in that prison where I was being held, but it was as though the very core of my soul wanted to do the right thing and follow the natural pull of the Universe. Then I felt my gran's energy guide me on my way, and in a moment's thought I was back in my body. I could see a cord of light floating from my stomach. This was the same cord I had seen when I had left my body, and as I watched it disappear, I felt my body come alive again and I felt a terrible depression enter my mind. I was a living human being again, and I was feeling with my body and mind yet again.

I lay there feeling again the cold and the physical pain. I felt a pair of evil hands keep shaking me and calling my name. I took one deep breath and gasped for air, and with that I could again feel the physical pain. I heard the evil voices say, 'She was out for a few minutes.' To me it felt I had spent hours in my spirit body. They said I was not breathing for a few minutes and told me that they had tried to revive me and bring me back. The words a 'few minutes' puzzled me, for I felt that I had spent a good five hours at least with my mum and at the stables and then with my gran. I then felt too much pain to think anymore. Surely, I thought, I must have been dreaming because I was so ill, but deep inside of me I knew that what I had experienced was no dream but had been real. I was indeed a spiritually minded person, but even if I had not been, I would still have known that what I had just experienced was very much real and more than a dream.

Chapter Three:
What the Spirit World Looks Like!

We all have our favourite place we like to go and see, maybe a beach abroad or even one that is near to home. It may be a place we haven't yet been to but have seen on our television screens, such as a mountain or the Great Pyramids of Egypt. We can see ourselves there and can even feel how it would be to go there. If it's a place we have already been to, we can imagine this far better than if we haven't been there before, but in any case we can see ourselves there, and it puts a smile on our face.

We all have our own unique way of thinking. To one person a place may look very beautiful; to another that place may look like the 'back end of a bus'. We all see things so differently, and that is why we are all unique and special in our own way. I often see people looking in the window of a travel agent's shop and say to the person next to them, 'God, would I love to go there!' I can see their faces light up when they talk about a beach abroad or a lovely hotel where they could go to relax.

For many people, their own home is a place of great beauty. It may be that they love where they live; they have spent much time and money making their home that special place to reside in, and they love being there. They enjoy coming in from work and relaxing there. Other people may find a city very beautiful. They may like to see large buildings standing tall in the view from their window or, like me, they may love to see the countryside and see the sea at its most glorious.

We are all so different. If we weren't, what a boring place the world would be! We sometimes want others to share our views, and maybe they sometimes do. We may want everyone to see beauty as we see it, and when they don't, we look at them blankly. A mother sees her baby as the most beautiful baby that has ever been born, while another mother may look and think that her baby is so much better. They say that beauty is in the eye of the beholder, and that is what I am trying to get at here.

When I first saw the Spirit World, it was just as I had imagined, only a thousand times better. I used to think that when I died, I would love to go to a place that was so green it would dazzle your eyes. I loved the countryside and all of nature, and I wanted so much to think that when I died, I would spend my spirit time in a place that reflected my love of the outdoors. I used to imagine it would be fields of green and skies of deep bright blue, and it would be just like that when I died.

I always had an image of this place in my mind's eye when my family would talk about people passing on to their next life. I knew it would be a place of great beauty, because my gran used to tell me, 'God's house is so nice, you would never want to leave.' She used to tell me that God could make the house just as you wanted it, and she would tell me that he could change the view in the blink of an eye. This puzzled me, so I asked my mother, who would come up with the answer, 'God's house has many mansions.' Again I would ponder on this, and when I was a young girl, I used to guess it meant that whatever we wanted, God could do, and so we would see whatever we wanted. I knew that there was a 'Heaven' (as I called it), and I always knew that it would be a great place and a happy place, just as so many people believe when they are young and talk about Heaven.

I was right about what I had expected, and in fact it was more beautiful than I had imagined as a small child. Now I want to tell you what I was shown of the Spirit World on this one occasion and what Spirit told me themselves about the World of Spirit.

I was just about to leave my physical body for the second time, and again I was feeling very lonely and sad. I could hear my heart pounding away, and I felt the same jerking feeling you have when you dream you are falling. I was used to this feeling, and I knew I was back in my Spirit Body.

This time I saw my physical body, and as I looked down on myself, I could see what had happened to me. I was in a very sorry state, and I felt a great feeling of anger as I looked at myself. I saw my face looking so pale and dull, as if it were reflected in a mirror. I could see that I had left my body and that the true me was free, but I just felt as though the energy that had been before was not like the loving one it had been. I felt it was so angry it could have destroyed something. I didn't know what to do with this energy. If I had been in my physical body, then I may have screamed or hit someone, but I wasn't in a body anymore; I was an energy.

I thought of those that had done this to me, and with that, I saw some objects in the room where my body lay start to fly around and break into nothing. There was a glass mirror in this room; it left the wall and fell on the floor with such force that it broke. I realised that it was my anger that had caused this. The angrier I became, the more things moved and broke like the mirror.

I then asked myself whether I wanted to stay feeling so angry and bitter. The answer was clearly no. I didn't want to stay here in this room; instead I wanted to be with my gran again, as I had been before when I had left my body. Perhaps other spirits would have taken the opportunity to stay in this place and seek some justice for what had happened to them. I knew all my upbringing had taught me much about the Spirit World, and I knew that it was better to be in a place of love and light and not grounded in a place that had taken my life. I knew that this was why so many souls stayed on the Earth and didn't move on. Some souls needed answers, and their energies needed healing. I knew they must find it so hard to let go and take the next step into the next life, and yet the anger in their energy caused them to feel grounded just as if they had still been in the physical body.

I then felt a warm feeling around me, and as I looked up with my spirit eyes, I could see my dear gran holding out her hand to me. I felt calm, and that feeling of love came back to me once more. I knew my gran would take care of me, and I felt the same glow of summer sun on my face as I had before.

She was smiling, but at the same time I could see her face was stained with tears. She was an energy like me, I know, but she had taken on her physical body so that I could recognise her and not fear her. She told me that she was also angry and that she wanted justice for what was happening. I asked her what we could do to get that justice, and with that she said, 'Follow me!'

She took me to a farm house that was really old and had an old coal fire in it. The room looked cosy and welcoming; it was the sort of place that I had wanted on Earth. I went to sit down on some cosy chair, and I felt like laughing. The fire was lit, and I could even hear the crackle of the coal against the heat. I asked my gran if this was Heaven, and she too started to laugh and said, 'Yes, it is your Heaven.'

'My Heaven, Gran?' I asked. I didn't know what she meant, and so I asked her.

She explained that this is where my spirit could recover and feel at home. She told me that the spirit was damaged and needed healing. She said that I was to stay where I felt happy and that I could have all what I wanted.

She added that I was in the place my spirit wanted to be and that every soul that enters the Spirit World needs to recover and accept its new form. She told me that because my spirit was damaged, I would need time to recover in a place of love and care, just like one would who was recovering from an illness on the Earth. She told me that every soul goes to a place that is comforting to them, a place where they can get used to being in their spiritual form. She told me that even the soul that passes on from life through natural causes still needs time to rest and gain that spiritual energy to make its journey onwards in the Spirit World.

My gran told me that I was to stay where I was happy and that whatever I wanted I could have, as long as it was pure and with good intent. I asked my gran why she was with me and why my other family members were not there. She answered that all I had to do was think of them and they would be 'everywhere'. She wore a smile just like the one I had known when she was alive. She seemed so full of joy and love, and I trusted every word she said.

I then chose to think of my pets who had long gone before me, and with that I heard a loud 'meow, meow'. I looked to my side and could see my pet cat Oliver, who had died when I was a child. He came to me with the same cry and purr that he had always had on Earth, and his body that in his last days had been so weak and frail now looked like that of a young kitten. He was young and fluffy and seemed so full of new life. He was the same Oliver, only much younger and vibrant and looking so happy and content. I went over to him and held him so tight that I didn't want to let go. He was so happy and content. I asked my gran why he looked so young now.

She told me that when all people and animals pass over to Spirit, they are in perfect form. No matter what has happened to their physical bodies before they died, all that would be gone in Spirit, and they would be able to manifest in whatever shape or form best suited them. She said that if someone had died of a terrible Illness or had lost a part of their body in some way, none of that would matter when they passed over, because they didn't need a body anymore. However, so that they could get used to this new energy form, they could choose to take on a physical form that would be just as they wanted and any age they chose. She told me that every soul has a personality just like on Earth, and like on Earth, we all have unique desires and needs.

I was so happy that she was telling me this. It made more and more sense of what was happening to me at that time, and I asked her more. I asked her what she looked like now and whether she was just standing before me like this so that I would be happy and not scared. She smiled and said to me, 'Do you want to see the real me?' I said yes, and with that my gran who stood before me had gone and in its place was something I shall never forget. I will do my best to describe this energy without adding in anything that wasn't there.

When we see a rainbow form in water or in the sky, it looks so effortless and stands with such beauty that we can't help but want to look at it. The energy of the Spirit looked like many colours entwined into one. It was like a small ball of fibre optic light shining on and off and glowing with such a brightness you would want to gasp. The ball of light was the size of a football. I tried to hold this energy ball, and with that it turned pink. This was the brightest pink you could imagine, and it hovered around my head. I felt such a warmth and love from this that I wanted it to stay there with me forever. The ball of energy then started to change shape, and with that my gran's physical form came back to me.

She smiled and asked me what I thought of what I had seen. I asked straight away if I could look like that, and she answered, 'You already do!' She told me that the ball of energy is the soul of man and animal and that the colours vary depending on the soul and its intent. She said that she had turned pink because that was the colour of love and care, and that is what she felt for me. She said that when we are alive in our body, we all have an aura, and this aura is what stays with us in our spirit form.

I was thinking of the Spirit World, and I asked my gran what I should do now. She told me that I needed to go outside and see the Spirit World and meditate to the 'Great Spirit'. I asked her what this meant, and she told me that she was still learning in the Spirit World and that she didn't hold all of the answers. She told me that she also needed to grow and develop even in spirit and that she had taken the task of caring for all the young children who had passed to Spirit quickly or through trauma. She told me that she had always adored children and she had wanted to help their souls once they came to Spirit, and this is what she was doing now. I had always known my gran loved children, as she was always there to care for them and attend them. She had taken care of six of her own children while on Earth and was always there for me and my sister when we were young, so I knew that she would always want to be around children, even in Spirit.

I asked her to come outside with me, and she did.

I went outside to see a beauty I will never forget. It would take your breath away! The flowers were about ten times bigger than ours, and the smell from them was stronger. They seemed so much brighter, and there was not a blemish on them. It was as if a gardener from a great place had attended to them and made them grow in ways that no human could do. The trees were in full bloom, and I could see valley after valley before my eyes. The sky was so blue it looked as though someone had taken a paintbrush to it. This place smelled of sweet roses and sweet Turkish delight! It was a smell that I have never smelt on Earth. I wanted to gaze and take it all in at once. It was like a scene from a painting. yet I was part of that scene as well.

I turned to see if my gran could tell me where to go next and she answered, 'Go in your soul, and you will find the right place.' I then felt myself floating above the land, and I felt a freedom that reminded me of the times spent when I went horse riding and would gallop for ages with the wind in my hair. I felt free and I could fly! I seemed to fly without effort, and I didn't know where I was going – only I felt I needed more information! I felt like I was free and didn't have a care about where to go – only that I wanted to take more and more of this place in.

It was a feeling of total peace; it was so natural and like nothing I had ever experienced in my physical life. I saw what looked like farms with animals grazing with one another. There were cows and sheep and horses. The horses caught my eye because I had always adored these animals. I can only describe them as horses that stood tall and proud. They were the brightest blacks and whites that you can imagine and their skins shone like no horse on Earth that I had ever seen. They were young and vibrant, and if there had been a horse like that on the Earth, I am sure that every horseman and woman would have wanted it.

With that, I saw what I can only describe as an angel. It was in the form of a woman with golden hair and wings so large they could hold about ten people in them. She had long golden hair, and her skin was pure white. She came to me with eyes that looked like those of a great eagle, and she spoke with a tongue that was so calming that I felt I could have followed her anywhere. She spoke in a way that I could understand, and she said to me, 'The Great White Spirit told me to come for you. You are not to come here yet. You are only allowed to stay for a short while, and I will take you back to Mother Earth.'

There was a warmth in her, and I was surprised because I had never imagined that an angel would look so large and so human. She was again like a painting on a canvas and so beautiful that anyone seeing her would have cried at the sight with tears of joy and hope.

I then thought of the terrible place I would have to go back to, and I tried to move away from this angel, I didn't want to return to Earth. I couldn't! The angel came to me and held me like a mother holds her child. She spoke to me like my mother would have spoken to me. She told me that I wasn't ready to leave the Earth yet and that the Great White Spirit had work for me. She said that I had chosen to go to Earth to do more work and that I had asked the angels to take me back so that I could carry out this work. She said that my work was being chosen for me and that from all of my suffering would come great rewards. She said that the evil in man does not go unnoticed and that through my suffering I would be able to serve others. She said that only those who suffer for the good of man can have such gifts.

I didn't understand what she was telling me, but I knew in my soul that what she said was true, and I knew that all of the pain I was going through was for a reason. I wanted to ask who the Great White Spirit was, but before I could do so, the angel answered, 'The Spirit of all is unconditional love and pure light that only certain souls are allowed to see. You will return to serve this love, and you shall in return see this love on your return.'

I had so much more to ask but, before I could do so, I was returned to my physical body that being handled by the evil ones once more. This time I felt no fear, and I felt like this hadn't been a dream. I knew this because the mirror that I had broken in my spirit form was still broken. There was someone standing over me saying I was a witch. They were scared as they were talking to each other and were commenting on the 'flying mirror'. They were saying, 'She was gone, out of it! How could she have done that?'

I knew the answer. I had been to the Spirit World.

Chapter Four:
What is God?

We find people divide into two groups when they are asked for their conception of God based on whether they have the personal idea of the Almighty Father or the impersonal. Both conceptions are right according to their level of spiritual knowledge.

The Christian and the Jewish religions have taken their idea of God from the Bible. In the Old Testament we read of Jehovah, God of the Hebrews and later accepted as God Almighty by the Christians, but here we have a God of Wrath, one who can be angered, who they say is a jealous God, and who does not hesitate to condemn conquered nations to be put to the sword. No mercy is shown to man, woman, child, or animal. However, the God of the New Testament is very different. The God of Jesus in the New Testament is a God of Love.

Unfortunately, Paul came a little later and gave this beautiful and true conception a twist which made God once again have a human failing, in as much as he could turn from his people and had to be reconciled by a human sacrifice in the form of the crucified saviour. In fact this is a pagan belief. Paul was born and bred in Tarsus where the pagan faith predominated, so it is not surprising that in his efforts to make his Christian God acceptable to the pagans, he adopted the idea of a crucified saviour.

Ever since human beings inhabited this Earth, there has always been at least one mind who could conceive ideas on a level a little above all others. In the beginning the intellect was animal, although the form was human; therefore the mind could not grasp spiritual thoughts. The leader had to try to persuade human beings to act differently – to bring a better idea of the humanities, not to be so cruel, not to be so eager to take life, and so on. Only after countless centuries could earthly minds be inspired with spiritual thoughts, and later still with special teachings. Today these minds are not so rare, and people are prepared to accept teachings from behind the veil. It is from such teachings that each soul can start to grow and progress.

When I was having all of these near-death experiences, I found that each time I came back from the Spirit World, I would have a more in-depth view of the many questions asked by people today relating to life and to God. It was as if I had received new wisdom and new teachings through my experiences that were given to me to bring back and share with all people on the Earth. I felt like I had a duty to do this and to use this knowledge for the good of all.

I feel that I was truly blessed with an insight in to the Spirit World that other people could only imagine or dream of. There are so many spiritual teachers and so many people telling us their idea of God and Spirit. They all provide a good foundation from which we can grow, and that foundation is knowledge. Humans have the need to grow and learn and seek answers to the many questions they hold from childhood onwards. It is part of the learning of us all. You will hear a child ask again and again, 'Why? But Why?' This comes from the soul's desire to grow and develop and learn more and more.

I was always told as a child that there is a God, and like many children I imagined that he sat in the clouds and sang hymns and had a long white beard. I always said my childlike prayers to this man in the clouds and tried to be on my best behaviour in order to make him happy and get him to like me.

Even as a child, I did find my image of God a little strange as, rather than seeing him as a kindly father, I felt there was still something not right about the way I felt for God. I felt that he was an angry man who could be easily upset, and if I upset him, then he wouldn't love me anymore. I felt that I needed more from this man, and as I grew older, I questioned my image of God, even wondering why he was a man and not a woman. Was it right that he had to be male, and why was this so? I felt like he was too human for my liking, and because of this, as I got older I started to look at other religions where their god or gods looked interesting and told a story about who they were and what we had to do to make them happy. I felt closer to these gods, because some of them didn't look human like my God, and they seemed to be on a more spiritual level, which I liked.

I didn't want a human man as a god, because I felt that there was no connection there and that this man could harm me when he wanted to, just as a human could.

So from a young age, I found myself not liking the God that I had always imagined. I still wanted to believe in a higher form to this life, but I didn't want it to be a human. I wanted something that made me feel warm and loved and cared for and something that I could understand and look up to.

I have always been interested in learning about other religions and never called myself a spiritualist. I felt that I didn't want a name tag like a designer bag, but I wanted to feel that I had a reason to be here and a reason to stay alive. I felt that my spiritual teachings gave me a good foundation to begin, because as a child I was always told that to be a spiritualist meant we are not part of a religion but a psychic phenomenon. I knew that I had a reason to be here, and I knew that there was a better place we all go once we leave Earth, but I still wanted to understand this God more and find out for myself who this God really was.

It wasn't until after my trauma and near-death experiences that I did find out some answers about God.

I felt that words were not needed to describe this God. I could feel his presence all around me once I came to the Spirit World. I felt that each time I was in Spirit, I could feel a higher form around me that was loving and caring and made me feel complete. It was the feeling you get when you are in love with someone and you can't stop thinking of them. They are in your head day and night, and they do not have to be with us for us to feel that love. We know it is there, because we feel it. We know we don't have to be with them to love them or for them to love us, for we feel it in our very being. It is also very much like a child at Christmas time. They know that there will be a Father Christmas coming to bring them gifts on Christmas Day, and they don't need to see Father Christmas to know he is there. They have to just feel it and know it is true, and from this feeling they get warmth and care.

All this is the feeling of love and faith, and that is what I was told by my spirit guides when I was with them. They told me that the finite mind cannot comprehend the infinite, it is impossible to form any mental image of God. God, they told me, is pure spirit and does not take on any form. He is pure light and pure love, and no man can imagine what he looks like, for he is a pure spirit.

God is love, light, and life – a supreme mind with wisdom and knowledge and justice and truth. Divine love, they told me, must not be confused with the earthly idea of love. No human can comprehend divine love if he confounds that divine quality with his human emotion, mingling as it does with possessiveness, jealousy, and lust. Divine love never changes under any circumstances whatsoever! It is eternal and has ever been and will ever be outpouring of itself upon creation.

But divine love is a quality that cannot be contained within itself. It is a quality that must be outpouring. Hence, if we try to find a reason for creation, I think we find it here. Love is incomplete without loving. Therefore the Almighty Spirit (God) created all things that his love may encompass them. In love were all souls created, and love influences the entire grand cycle of Spirit's evolution.

I feel that my time in Spirit gave me the answers to my many questions about God. I had discovered now that he was a divine spirit that did not have a physical form. God was not male or female, was not animal or anything that took form or name. This spirit was the Great White Spirit of all man and soul.

Spirit told me that man contains many images of what God looks like, but if we take a look at some of those images, we see why man's mind was inspired to make them so.

Many of the images, including the Christian one that many children still imagine and are shown in drawings, depict a man who looks very much like a father. That is why some Christians call him the 'Great Father'. When we think of a father, we think of someone that will love us or take care of us and protect us from harm, and this is exactly what the Great White Spirit will do and what he is all about. It is man's way of trying to give an image to a feeling, to something we know is there but can't see and therefore need to imagine. It is just like man sees love. He knows it is there, but he needs to give it a symbol that represents the feeling. So to put an image to it, he may draw a heart, as this is where man feels love – from the heart.

It is the same with other religions. Some may have many gods and goddesses, and each one will look different and have a different side of the Great White Spirit that they want to try to express.

Spirit told me that no religion was right or wrong; each one took what is true for every man and soul, and that was an idea of how we need to live and progress in life. We are all Spirit. We each strive to feel love and truth and wisdom, and these are contained within what the Great White Spirit (God) is made up of. Each religion will teach us what we need to know as a soul progressing. For a soul to progress, it will often find knowledge by being drawn to certain religions and certain people. Take the case of a man who wishes to be a monk all his life. The monk leads a simple life, and the main aim of his day is meditation and prayer. This soul may need to feel this peace and learn to go inward and seek its own connection with God by doing this. So it is that every man will be drawn to the way they want to see God and to what is best for them. No one is wrong, as we all have a path that is right for us, and at the end of this life we all go to the Divine Great Spirit which is pure love and light.

Some people may have no religion, and this is not wrong, for some people who say they have no faith in anything are people who are very spiritual and don't know it. I have met many who say they have no faith, and they are such loving people. They are kind and caring and show more of the ways of a good soul than many of those who are seen as great spiritual leaders.

I knew that spirits were telling me that we are all so different and our souls have different reasons for being on this Earth. They told me that we all carry the gift of love and care and that we are all part of the Great White Spirit (God). We are all one, and each of us belongs to God. We do not have to have a faith to know there is a divine spirit, for each of us connects to this spirit whether we like it or not!

I felt that all the time I was in the Spirit World, I was given the feeling of the Great White Spirit. In my case, I always felt a beautiful love that felt so unconditional. It was like no love I had felt before, and I knew that I was closer to this divine energy. Spirit told me that the Great White Spirit was with me in my time of pain and trouble and that I only had to think of that pure love for that divine spirit to be with me. It was a great energy that is difficult to describe. I needed to be able to describe it, and it was as if I needed to share that love with everyone else and express that same feeling that I had felt. I knew it would make me a more loving person, for its feeling was so great that I knew I was given it to share with others.

I was also told that the Great White Spirit has so much love to give us that it will bring certain souls to the Earth to show this love and its teachings. That is why we were given great teachers such as Jesus Christ and others that came to the Earth. They were given to man so that he may feel this divine love and see its light and power and to show us that we are all loved by the Great White Spirit.

My near-death experiences increased my knowledge of God, so it became clearer to me what the Great Spirit is like. I felt very lucky and privileged to be given this understanding so early on in my life.

I now feel that the Great Spirit is everywhere and is mostly found in the quality of love that we all share. We all seek out a lover or at least a friend we can love, and little do we know that this is because we all belong to the Great White Spirit, who has given us great love that joins us all.

Chapter Five:
Leazare and Spirit Guides

I was told that every living soul on the Earth has a spirit guide. From the moment we are born, we are given a soul that will be our guide and friend while we are on Earth.

This soul will *never* leave us, no matter what we do in life or who we turn out to be. Throughout this life, we are all going to have this friend remain with us. We are all unique, and so are our spirit guides. We are born with this right which is a natural law of life. No person can take this guide away from us.

When we are still in Spirit waiting to be born, we are given a guide that will be born with us. This guide is usually a more advanced soul who has attained a higher order in life. The guide has worked in Spirit to become wiser and a kind of teacher and the guide's wish is to return to help other souls. This guide may be a friend or family member from a past life, but one thing is for sure: this guide is a soul whose intentions are good and of 'light'. It doesn't matter what the person they are serving is like. The guide will only see the light and the good in us all and will only try and guide us with their own love and light.

We have many spirit guides who will watch over us and serve us on Earth; they will be there to help us when we need help and offer us unconditional love and care. We also all have a main guide that is called our 'door keeper'. To be a door keeper, that spirit must be of a higher realm, and to be a 'light worker' is to serve Spirit. Its knowledge of Spirit must be so advanced that it has progressed in its life to serve others. Its purpose is to protect us from any negative influences or thoughts that can harm our soul. The door keeper is a strong soul that can defend us when we are being attacked both physically and spiritually, because it has a power that is used for the good of man and life on Earth.

Some souls that come back to Earth are already themselves very advanced and what some would term 'old souls'. This means that they themselves are 'advanced light workers' and have gained a knowledge of Spirit; they decide to be reborn and use this knowledge for the good of others. This soul may be a great teacher or even a simple soul that only works in a shop, but their love and care on the Earth is valued, and they have great gifts that they share in many ways with others. It may only be the 'gift of love' to others or a person who has a way with words that can help heal others.

These souls are usually born with door keepers who are a very advanced souls and are themselves old souls. These door keepers may be of an 'angelic realm', and they come to Earth to help that person further with their soul journey.

These door keepers are like our best friends. They check to see if we are safe and well, and they try to inspire us and guide us. One thing they will never do is make choices for us. They are not allowed to stand in our way of learning on this Earth, and even though they can inspire our thoughts to do a certain thing or act in a certain way, they cannot and would not want to stand in the way of our personal progress. They show us unconditional love and care, similar to that shown by a mother to her child, and they only try to help and guide us on our way in life.

They do not expect us to find out about them. They are there even if the person doesn't believe in them. If we do find out about them and then use that knowledge to help in our lives, well all I will say is 'Wow!' They then come to us even stronger than before, and the help and support we can get from them is one hundred times stronger. It is a love relationship that is the natural law of life. This guide will even be there for us when we are in Spirit, and they may keep coming back to Earth with us a number of times.

I was always told by my mum and gran that our guides are given to us according to what we need to learn on this Earth. You may have heard about guides, and you may hear people say they have a nun or a Native American Indian as a guide. We all have guides that have advanced in their ways and their knowledge of the Spirit World. You may ask why we have guides or door keepers who are nuns or Native Americans. Well, it is because these souls have knowledge from Earth about spiritual ways of living that they have taken with them to another life. On the Earth they learnt how to meditate and how to use the energy of the Earth. When they have passed on to Spirit, they have maintained their knowledge. They then want to use this teaching to help others, and so that is why many mediums have guides that are souls like this.

I always knew I had spirit guides, and I always knew some of them by name. I was told by my gran about two of them. She told me when I was young that I had a little girl with me called Pavinder; she was a Hindu girl, who had passed to Spirit when she was about twelve years of age. She told me that I would always have her in my life and that she would come to me in the form of a child because this is how she was happy. She told me that Pavinder has long black hair and that she brought me spices and herbs that I would be able to smell when she was around.

I did dream of this girl when I was younger. When I was sick, I would smell herbs and spices around me, and so I knew she was near. I asked my gran why she had come to me, and my gran told me that she felt I had known her in a past life and that she wanted to remain my friend. I started to dream more of this girl, and I even started to see her by me on many occasions. I would be sitting playing with my cars (yes, I was a tom boy) and then I would see an Asian child asking to join in. I would shout to my mum and tell her that my friend wanted to stay for tea. I think my mum just thought this was an imaginary friend.

Children do see spirits and often will say they have a friend, and their parents think that this is just child's play with an invisible friend. Sometimes years later, if you asked the child about this friend, they will say they sensed a child or friend near them who they believed to be real – and they are real; it is Spirit.

My guide and main door keeper is called Leazare. He has been with me since birth, and I used to have vivid dreams about him from the age of ten. I would dream I was in a large castle watching a man in a long black gown practicing a lot of magic. I would see pots lifting in mid-air and other objects being lifted at the will of this man. It was very much like a scene from Harry Potter! I would look on and would see a young blonde-haired lady who would be standing next to him as he seemed to be teaching her these magic tricks. She would be looking on in amazement as I, as a ten-year-old child, was spellbound by his actions.

In my dream, this man would turn around and see me. Then he would hold out his hands to me in a peaceful way, asking me to come over to him. His eyes were so dark but so kind and gentle, and I always felt safe in that dream as I went over to him, and he would wrap his gown around me and make me feel warm and safe. I would dream of this man often as a child, and then as I got older, I would have more and more vivid dreams of him, and I would hear him speak to me in a foreign tongue. It seemed to sound like German, but at the time I had no idea what language was being spoken.

I used to love the castle he was in. it was full of magical-looking objects, and there was an aroma in the air of fresh herbs and flowers and nature. I would walk around the castle, and as the years went by and I grew older, I found myself turning into the young blonde-haired lady who stood by him and learnt from him. I would see myself next to him and know that I felt so much love and passion for him, and I would look on so eagerly to learn his teachings – what he was showing me about white magic and how to heal people. He taught me about nature and all things of the spiritual way. When I was about seventeen, I dreamt of this man night after night. He never told me his name, but we seemed so close, and when I awoke I would describe them to my mother, who would tell me he was a guide from Spirit there to help me.

It was not until I was nineteen and having my near-death experiences that I found out his name and who he was and why he was there to help me. I first learnt all about him when I had my third near-death experience. I was about to leave my body once again, when I saw the man whom I had dreamt of all those years. He held out his hand to me, and as I took hold of it in my eagerness to be rescued, I remember him taking me into his black gown and lifting me up into his strong arms. He towered above six foot and was of a medium build but very strong, and he lifted me as if I was a feather. I saw tears streaming down his face, and he spoke in the foreign tongue that he had spoken in my dreams. I still had no idea what he was saying.

He then carried me with him in his arms to the castle. Once there, he faced me and spoke again in the foreign tongue. I stood and stared at him and wanted so badly to know what it was he was saying. I got so eager that I shouted to him, 'I can't understand you!'

With that, he smiled and remained silent. Then he began to speak to me in a language I could understand – good old plain English. The first words I remember were, 'I love you.' I was so touched by the words, and I felt such warmth coming from them. He held my hand and spoke to me with such love and care, and I listened intently to every word.

He told me what I had waited years to hear, and that was his name,

Leazare. He repeated it twice and asked me to say it back to him. I repeated the name, and as I did so, memories came flooding back to me. The images were so clear that suddenly I knew that he was my dear friend whom I had lost all those years ago. I remembered the castle and the smells and the way he would touch me and hold me and the way he had tried to save my life when I was being put to death. Yes, I was remembering the life I had shared with him, and all the memories were coming to me of the way we had been and what had parted us in the end.

Leazare was a German count of the sixteenth century who lived in Germany, and he had lived as what we would today term a wizard or a witch. He would carry out white magic and spells, and he would help heal people who came to him for all health problems and worries through his knowledge of herbs. He would mix herbs and give them to people. He was born a healer and had the gift of understanding very old magic that he would often practice. He lived in this castle alone and was very wealthy by today's standards. He worked alone as well and didn't care much for company, apart from the many animals that inhabited the castle with him.

I met Leazare by accident while I was a young woman who was hiding from her village as an outcast, because I refused to live how they lived. In fact, I was a bit of a rebel. I didn't want to be like my family and kill people and fight and follow a religion I didn't want to know about, so I decided to run away from my home and find my own way.

I was cold and hungry and had nowhere to go. I had travelled miles on foot, and I wanted so badly just to sleep and find a shelter. I came upon the castle, and despite fearing what may be inside it, I wanted to rest. So when my tired and weary body came to a stop outside its large dark door, I found the courage to knock upon it. The light was so dim that I found it difficult to see, and I had to squint at the large figure that towered over me and asked me what I wanted.

I must have fainted, because the next thing that I remember is being on a warm bed and being attended to by this solemn-looking man. He was lifting my head so I could drink, and I did drink as I was so thirsty.

He cared for me in my weak state for a number of days, and when I had regained my strength and power, I started to sit up and speak with him. He never said much, but after a while he seemed to trust me and told me about himself and his name and what he did in the castle. He also questioned me about my state and where I had come from and why I was so ill and weak. I must have clammed up and said that I didn't wish to answer. He didn't question anymore and said that he already knew and that he would let me stay there for as long as I needed and that then I would have to return.

This alarmed me, so I jumped up and asked him what he knew. As I demanded this, he could hear the great pain in my voice. He sat down by me and touched my hand and said, 'I see into your heart and soul, and I see pain and fear, and I see isolation. The rest fits into place. You are escaping from people who are not like you.' He then just stood up and walked off.

I began to get up so I could follow him, but then I realised that I was naked! In a fit of temper, I raged out loud that he had no right to see me naked, and how dare he undress me. With that, he came back to me and told me to be still, as I was still very weak. I shouted that he was rude and had no right to undress me. He then did something I had never seen him do all the time I was there being cared for by him; he smiled and laughed at me. This made me angrier, but the more I showed my anger, the more he would laugh. I calmed myself and told him I was leaving. With that, he reached out and said, 'I don't see flesh. I see a spirit that is walking around in a cell and is in need of care.' When I heard his words, I calmed down and began to smile back at him. He looked at me and said, 'You can come and help me and see what I do.'

He took me to a room full of pots and bowls that were filled with what looked like herbs and liquids. He held my hand to steady me, and I felt like he was my friend and that I was safe with him. After such a long time of feeling lonely, I started to feel happy and believe that I had a reason to live.

Leazare showed me all the magic that he performed, and he told me that there was a cure in nature for every Illness and disease and that we only had to look to find a cure, and after some faith and care we could be healed of anything. He told me that even the mind can be healed with the right herb.

He never mixed the herbs with just his physical hands, but he also mixed them with white magic, which he said we can all learn and find in nature. Leazare would call upon the elements and use fire, Earth, air, and water in all he did. He told me that the secret to all his medicines was to mix in his own love and passion to help the person heal.

I would watch him mix herbs and chant spells, and I remember being there in that castle for a long time and learning much from him about the white magic and the laws of the Great Universe. I would see things fly in the air and objects move on their own, and I would see him make lights appear from nowhere in a room.

Weeks had passed, and he wanted to teach me some of what he did. We found that we both had formed a loving bond and cared for each other. I was just young, and he was so much older than I, but we were becoming close, and we enjoyed each other's company, so we would spend all our time learning from each other. I found his ways were the ways that were truly in my heart, and I wanted to never leave him, as I found myself falling deeply in love with him.

I lived there for a long time, and one day while I was out, one of my family members saw me leave his castle and followed me. They saw me picking herbs and chanting spells as I went about my day. This family member reported what he had seen to the rest of my family and told them I was a witch and was using black magic. My family already believed that I had disgraced them by leaving the family home, and they were so annoyed at hearing about my activities that they gathered together a mob of people and set out to find me.

They found me as I left the castle, and again I was followed – this time by a mob of people ready to take my very life from me. They grabbed me and dragged me kicking and screaming back to the village for a trial. They felt I was an outcast and that I had done wrong in leaving them and not following their orders. They accused me of being a witch and said that I should be put to death.

There was no trial, but it was decided that I should be burnt at the stake for being a witch. I was beaten until I was unaware of my surroundings, and then all I can remember was the flames growing stronger and brighter around me.

I was screaming and in pain, but at that moment I felt a large hand hold me by the shoulder and pull me free. It was Leazare. He had found me and risked his own life to set me free. Some of the men from the village tried to stop him, but his strength both of body and mind was such that no one could prevent him saving me.

He carried me on his back to a place where he laid me down and tried to heal me. It was too late, though, as the very life force was draining from me and I was ready to leave my body. The fire had done its damage, and I was hanging on to a thread of life. Leazare took me in his arms, and I saw the anguish in his face as his soul mate was taken from him. I remembered all he said in those final moments, especially these words: 'I love you and I will always be by your side. I will follow you here life after life, and I will always be there when you say my name.' With that, my soul was free to make its journey to the Spirit World.

Leazare didn't live long after that, as he wanted to be with me so badly, and he died of a broken heart. He wanted to remain by my side, as he felt he couldn't be without me, so he joined me in the Spirit World.

I know that Leazare follows me always. and he is my main guide that I know will always be here for me on Earth and in Spirit. He is a very advanced soul, and he resides on a higher realm. I have had many mediums and psychics tell me about him and how he is near me. They all say that he is from a higher realm, as he comes with a light so bright it would blind the naked eye. I feel very lucky to have Leazare, as I feel that he helps me progress on my journey and helps me when I most need it. I always feel him near me, and when I do my spiritual work, I feel him by my side, and he helps me know that I must help others and use my gifts to do so.

When I had my third near-death experience, it was Leazare who came to me and showed himself again to me. After all the memories came back to me about our time together, he then spent time with me talking to me and telling me he would never leave me. He told me that he wanted me so badly to stay with him, but he said that I would have to return to Earth to use my many gifts to help other people.

It was Leazare on this third near-death experience who told me about my time on Earth. He told me that I had many gifts that I could use to help others. He told me that I had been to the Earth many times and that I had learnt more and more over time that had made me become a more advanced soul. He said I was to help others and go back and finish my work there.

I wanted to know why I was going through all this pain and suffering. How could this happen if I was meant to help others? He told me that I would gain more knowledge because of it, and I would go on to save many others from the same kind of suffering. He told me I had a job to do in opening the eyes of people to what needed to be done to stop this suffering.

He said that during each lifetime, I had a path that would not be easy and that I had chosen to follow this path to make sure that I was helping other souls. He told me that this lifetime would be my last on Earth but that I must complete the journey I had set out on.

He held me with love and passion and care, and I knew that we were bonded in Spirit. I wanted to remain with him in the Spirit World, which I felt was my true home, but I knew again in my heart that this was not the time for me to stay.

Leazare told me that I had to go through this experience in order that

I could follow my true path. He said that I needed to help others see the truth of life and spread the fact that we all live on and we are all Spirit that will never die. He said I would obtain more gifts of seeing spirit now that I had been to the Spirit World, and he said that through my pain and suffering I would become a stronger and more powerful healer.

Now I was beginning to understand why I had to suffer so much. Experiencing pain would help me realise that I had a job to do in helping others on Earth and others who were about to leave their physical body to go to the Spirit World. I felt that my soul had awoken to its real purpose on the Earth, and it gave me such a peaceful feeling to know the true reason for all my pain at that time.

Leazare had given me the wisdom to know there was a meaning for the wrong being done to me and that I had to use what I had learnt to go on and serve others and serve spirit.

I stayed with Leazare for what seemed a lifetime. Then he repeated that I was ready to go back to my body and help others. This time I had a reason to return. I had been given many answers to my many questions, and I felt that I had awoken to my gifts. Now I knew I was a worker for spirit and I had a job to do. It was still difficult to leave Leazare and return to my body, but I trusted Leazare and Spirit, and I had a deep feeling that they wouldn't let me down.

On this occasion I was taken back to my body in a different way. Leazare carried me back in his arms as if I were a child. I felt my life force return to me as I woke and took a gasp for air and found myself back in my body.

Chapter Six:
Journey to Learn the Answers of Life

There was to be one final occasion when I visited the Spirit World, where not only did I see loved ones, but I found the answers to the many questions asked by humans. This time I was not in the evil place where I had been tortured, but I was free and at home with my loving mum and all my beautiful animals around me. I had escaped from the army and was now back home trying to build a life for myself and trying to feel human once more.

I was free from the army and its abuse, but I still had the mental scars from my experience of torture. For this reason, I felt I was not free from the mental scars it had caused me, and I was still living a life of pure hell. This was reflected in the illness of my mind that was causing me to become very low in body and spirit.

I felt trapped in my mind, and no one could get through to me, I was unable to function as a human. I was just living day to day and trying to cope with so many bad memories. My dear mum tried her best to help me. She would hold me night after night as I went through the terrible nightmares and pain of all that had happened to me. She was always telling me to hold on to life and try to look forward, but telling me that just wasn't sinking in, and I was growing more and more depressed.

This depression nearly took my life. I was on medication and would take it regularly, but the terrible depression continued. Within me, I still held memories of the Spirit World, and I felt tempted to return to my true home. I wanted to escape from the human mind that held so much pain and suffering. Deep down, I was aware that I had always kept hold of the memories of the Spirit World, and it was these memories and what I had learnt that made me want to go back to my true home and find my escape from my human mind that held so much pain and suffering. I knew deep down that Spirit had told me I was not meant to come back to the Spirit World yet, because I still had work to do, but I wanted so badly to escape the pain by returning to my spirit form.

With that in mind I did take too many pills in the hope that I could go back to my favourite place and be with those I loved. I was scared in some ways in case it didn't work, but it seemed worth the risk to experience the Spirit World again. I just wanted so badly to get those memories back and make them real once more.

I must have been near death's door again. As I lay on my bed alone, I could see the transparent cord that attached me to this world. I saw it growing stronger and stronger, and I knew that I was ready to leave my body again. I knew that I was not to come back to Spirit yet, but I wanted to be in a place that was free from pain and where my bad memories would disappear.

Over my bed, there was a lovely light shining over me which began to grow larger and larger. It was like a bright sunny day, yet again giving me a sense of calm that made me feel happy that I was going to be in the Spirit World with all this beauty. Once again, the light turned into my dear gran. She came to me and held me as she had always done on Earth. She was looking at me with so much love and concern. She told me that I was not meant to come back with her yet, but she knew I needed healing and help. She had come to take me to Spirit to teach me some things that I could keep with me in my Earth life and use when I needed to. Gran told me she would take me on a journey to help me to see the work I had to do on this Earth. This would help me to heal so that I could become the person I was meant to be and to do the work for Spirit and the Great White Sprit.

During this experience, I was taught some lessons about life that I want to share with you now. They help to answer the many questions about this life and beyond, that every human being asks and has been asking for years and years.

My gran took me by the hand and kissed me on the forehead and told me that she would take me with her for a short time and let me see the work ahead of me. She took me back to the farm house where she had taken me before. I could see the large fire yet again and experience the warmth of the place that made me feel secure and loved. My gran sat down by my side and told me that this would be my last time here until my rightful time, which would be made clear by the Universe itself. She told me that I had work to do on Earth before I would be able to come to my rightful place. My gran said that she would show me more of the Spirit World and teach me things that I could then go on and use for the good of others.

My gran took me outside to the beauty of the Spirit World and she told me that I must heal; I must take in the beauty of the Spirit World and realise that I have a reason to go back and live a good life that would all lead to me one day returning. I looked around and saw the beauty of the flowers yet again. I could smell them as though I was in a sweet shop full of delights and smells that make you smile and make you want to breathe in more and more. I touched the flowers and they felt like silk, as they were so soft to the touch. It was an amazing feeling! It was a sight that would make you believe in a better life. It was a small miracle that seemed like a large one to me! This was the beginning of my discovering more about this world, and I wanted to take in as much as I could before I knew I had to return to Earth.

Not far from the flowers, I could see what looked like a dragonfly. It moved around gracefully. Its colours were so bright and illuminating that it seemed to light everywhere as it flew. I watched it in amazement and knew that it was small things like this that made me see the Spirit World as a place full of amazement and miracles. If everyone could see just one of these, they would all believe in this better life and know that we are all here for a reason and that we all will live this beautiful life once we are in our spirit shoes.

My gran told me that I could meet all of my family and see anyone that I wanted to see. She told me that all I had to do was think of their love and I would see them.

An important part of my life is spent with my animals, and I was always someone who thought of my animals as the main thing in my life. As each one of them passed on to the Spirit World, I would always place them in the garden with a cross or a crystal to help them on their journey. I was always told by my family that my animals would surround me and be with me once I passed on to the Spirit World, and guess what? They were! I could see all of them the moment I thought of them. I could see all of my cats and rabbits and hamsters – even the horses that I had ridden as a young girl that had now passed on to Spirit. It was as though they were all coming towards me, and as each one passed by me, I had the opportunity to hold them and feel that beauty and love we had always shared. I was amazed how perfect they all were. One of my cats called Sammy had lost his tail on Earth, but now his tail was all perfect just as it had been before his accident.

This was an experience that I will never forget. It was wonderful to have the opportunity to say hello and feel them close to me as I had before. It was also very comforting to know that they were all safe and well and that they all seemed happy in their little lives.

I also thought of my other family members, my grandfather and my auntie and all my other dear loved ones who had passed on to spirit. As I thought of each one, I could see them! They all seemed to wear a smile, and each of them came to me with open arms and love. I wanted to take them all in and study each of them in turn. It was like one big party together after years of being apart. They all seemed so happy and full of life, and they all seemed to have the same personalities that they had on Earth. My auntie had been a lady that was 'full of fun', and she had always joked and made people laugh. She came to me and held me in her arms and began telling me some amusing jokes. It was as if I was at home with all those people I cared about and adored. I could see my grandfather had a farm. He had always been a farmer on Earth, and I knew he would one day go to Spirit and still care for animals and land. This was what he was doing now. He was caring for the land and making sure he grew the finest vegetables available. He wanted me to go with him to the farm and see all he had grown and all of the animals in his care.

It was as if I had been given this time to take in the entire Spirit World and make sure I had happy memories to take back with me and share with others. My grandfather took me by the hand, and the next thing I knew I was on this large piece of farmland that seemed to be miles and miles long. He showed me the vegetables he was growing, and when I bent down to take a look I could see they were potatoes. He took one from the ground, and I could smell the dirt so fresh and sweet. It was the largest potato I have ever seen, and I was so surprised that I gasped and stood back. My grandfather smiled at me and told me that he loved to grow food. I asked him why spirit had to eat food, and with that he sat down and asked me to sit next to him. He said that he would tell me one of the many secrets of the Spirit World so that I would know why it was they still grew food and were able to eat it.

My grandfather told me that on Earth many people starve and have no food. He said that man had been given the means to grow all the food they ever needed, but they sometimes didn't have the knowledge or the right conditions to do this. He said that food was the fuel for every human being and that it was a part of life that no man could live without. Even small children come to this world and starve before they have even had the chance to taste food.

He told me that it was the universal right that every man should eat food. He enjoyed growing things while he was on Earth, and he enjoyed eating what he had grown. He said that it was like the little coal fire I had seen before on my visit to the Spirit World. I had seen that coal fire because it helped me to feel safe and secure while my spirit had healed. He said it was the same as the land he loved in spirit. He had chosen to grow things so that the people and children who came to the Spirit World who had not had much to eat, would have the chance to taste food and know what it was like. He told me that even though the soul doesn't need food, just as I didn't need that coal fire, it was a way for the soul to heal and experience the next stage of their healing process.

He told me that he loved to grow food and see souls experience the feel of it and the pleasure of it. He had even made sweets for the children to taste and experience the true delights of being a child. He said that the land was for growing good food for the soul and that it also helped him to learn to meditate and feel closer to the Great White Spirit.

My grandfather told me that all souls need to experience the Spirit World in their own time and in a way that they can accept. They must be able to learn about themselves being an energy and not a solid form anymore. He said that time in Spirit is not a thing anymore. He said that time was only something that was needed on Earth. Time was not important in the Spirit World, and what seemed like hours to me on Earth might only seem like a second to those in spirit. This explained why I always felt I had spent hours in Spirit when in fact it may have only been a few minutes.

I was told that when we are on Earth and a loved one passes over, time to them is not a problem anymore. They no longer need to be a servant to time, and the only thing to rule that soul is free will. I was told that it is like the wife who passes to the Spirit World before her husband. He may feel he had to wait years and years to be with her, and this time may seem like forever, but for the wife in Spirit that time may only seem like a few hours.

There were two lessons here about the Spirit World and two things I had learnt about the way we are when we pass over to Spirit. I had been told many things before like this about Spirit – how they have things they like to help them heal and get used to their new form and about how time didn't matter in Spirit – but to hear them from someone in the Spirit World and understand them better was confirmation for me that they were real and had real meaning.

These were not the only things I learnt about the Spirit World. I was given this last time to learn so much more, and I will now pass the knowledge on to you about each thing I learnt one by one.

Chapter Seven:
Reincarnation

While I was in the Spirit World, I was able to see one of my past lives. Leazare took me to a woodland where I saw the remains of an old helicopter. I wondered why he was showing me this and what this had to do with me being in the Spirit World. All I could see around me was wreckage and burnt-out bits of this helicopter. It was like a scene from a film where you see the remains of a crash and the person is looking around and taking in all that is around them.

I asked Leazare to explain why he was showing me this scene, and he said, 'This is the way you came here before in one of your earthly lives. You were a helicopter pilot and had an accident when the helicopter you had flown in crashed and brought you over here.' Leazare went on to tell me about this other life and gave it the name that is known to us all – reincarnation.

Some people who believe in reincarnation say that we must return again and again to the Earth to experience all the conditions of life on Earth, assuming that a mind cannot be evolved until it has known the life of the wealthy, the poor, the hard working, the lazy, and so on. Leazare told me that all souls come to Earth again and again if they wish to. He told me that this is the way that a soul can learn lessons that will help their soul to progress more and more into their spiritual journey. Leazare also told me that it was also emphasised most strongly that the return of the spirit to the Earth was a voluntary act on the part of the spirit. There was no universal law compelling any soul to return to the Earth, either once or over and again, as is believed by some.

It is alleged that Buddha passed through three thousand reincarnations. If this is the fact, then he did so of his own free will. Every soul is given freedom of will to progress in their spiritual life. When the term 'free will' arises, it is usually associated with normal life and appears to be a misnomer when one considers that there is frustration from every direction. The Great White Spirit gave us all free will that we may decide whether to love him or reject him as we choose, and this free will is a gift that can be exercised on all planes of life except on Earth, where it is more limited. Free will from a loving God would be an unworthy gift, for who would want to experience pain and struggle, hardship, and misery? However, it is those difficult lessons that we must endure if we are to achieve strength of character and a sympathy and an understanding for others in their mental and physical trials. We are never expected to control entirely our outer conditions of life on Earth, but the free will that counts and that is all important lies within the inner life of man. Whatever circumstances or environment surround him, it rests with him alone how he reacts to the life that meets him each day.

Free will of thought may seem a poor substitute for free will of action, yet it is the more important of the two. It is thought that builds the character and personality and shapes the inner body. Thought prepares us for the life to come; thought ensures whether we shall be loved or hated, held in esteem or despised. It is fortunate for mankind that only limited free will extends beyond the realms of thought, because otherwise we should become even more selfish then we are; we have only to look at the world today to realise how even our limited free will is abused and misused.

In spirit there are no restrictions, and what each of us believes to be the best for the spirit's progress can be obtained by wishing, for thought is creative of one's conditions. This freedom of action does not always mean progression, It can mean regression. During an earthly life, certain men and women live decently and within the law because they are frightened by the fear of being hurled into Hell if they live otherwise. They are not moral and decent people by preference but only behave well because they fear the consequences of Hell. Then they pass to spirit and discover that there is no man on a throne meeting out punishment or reward to suit the case of each newly arrived spirit. That is when their true spirit shines through and they will have the will to progress at their free will because they want to and not because they fear.

Spirits who are newly freed from their physical bodies can be so contented and satisfied in every way with their life on the astral planes that they may not even contemplate reincarnation. It may be a matter of a century or centuries before they come to the conclusion that the way they are does not give the best opportunities to overcome a certain weakness or fault. Earth life is such a great school with lessons every hour! It is a cramming school, where so much can be done in such a short while – short in comparison to eternity.

One argument frequently used by those who do not want to return to Earth is that although we are supposed to come back for a specific reason, we are utterly unconscious of it. A few can achieve glimpses of previous lives, but these are the exceptions and are rare. It is true that we are none of us conscious of any previous life. Life appears to have started when we took the first breath after birth, yet apparently we have come back for the most important purpose, our own well-being. How can we achieve this end when we are not conscious of it?

The conscious mind knows only a fraction of all the knowledge stored in the spirit's mind. When we are asleep, the normal brain is not in action, but the larger mind of the spirit never goes out of action, and it is during the sleep state that the spirit can review its body's daily life and decide what impressions it must 'get through' next day to its normal consciousness. The spirit, knowing the whys and wherefores of its reincarnation, will cause ideas to arise during the daily life, and the conscious mind accepts these ideas and acts upon them, thus bringing out the reason for the new life on Earth. Some people may have no idea why they have a desire to do this or that, and the full realisation will not come until they are free from the limitations of this body and back in the Spirit World.

It may be argued that it would be a lot more reasonable if we could remember the past life and the purpose for the return. It would simplify matters, and we could set about righting the wrong or whatever it was we had come back to Earth to do. That sounds a good argument, but there is an equally strong one against it. To make the most of the opportunities this present life offers us, there must be no bias pulling our minds this way or that way. If we could remember our former lives, we would naturally make comparisons all the time, and we should not be able to accept this present life as normally as we do. Supposing this life were a great improvement on the last, then remembering the troublesome times from which we had escaped, there might be a danger that we would take the credit for present circumstances with a sense of satisfaction that can amount to pride in having accomplished the reward of these improved conditions. Pride can hinder the soul's progress. On the other hand, supposing this present life were one of financial difficulties and illness and we remember the former life as having money and great health, our mind would want that back and keep going over it.

Without memories of a past life, we can progress through our next incarnation and enjoy the smaller pleasures in this life. Forgetfulness is best. We take our trials and our times of happiness as they come, with no biased memory making endless comparisons.

Earthly experiences are only necessary in as much as they give the required lessons. One spirit may progress more quickly than another and reach that stage when more earthly lessons are not essential. The other spirit may learn more slowly, and in this case the training may require the taking on of bodies placed in greatly contrasting aspects of earthly life. However, it is the spirit training that is required, not innumerable experiences of contrasting lives. These are only given as lessons until the goal is reached.

Reincarnation is more generally accepted by those spirits who have progressed just beyond the astral, and having entered the spiritual realms there is a greater awareness of their faults and how far they lack perfection.

If we can picture a garden badly overgrown with weeds, it would be difficult to distinguish one weed from another in the mess. Then along comes the gardener to pull up the weeds, leaving the flowers to be seen in their beauty. But here and there some weeds have been overlooked, and just because there are only a few of them, they are all the more conspicuous. So it is with our faults; the fewer we have, the more we realise that they exist.

When the spirit has attained to a still higher evolution, it may overcome its remaining defects without a physical life, but in some cases such an advanced soul may wish to return to the Earth to help mankind in many ways. The thought vibrations radiating from its mind irrespective of the lowly body it may inhabit; would inspire the thoughts of all of those people whom it met.

Until a soul has evolved to a considerable degree, it cannot afford to lose the lessons learnt on Earth. Pain, hardship, misery, and all evil are severe taskmasters, but in the end they have produced a spirit that is generous in love, patience, and tolerance, and that is strong in character.

In spirit each soul reviews its own past, with its sins and omissions, and it then comes to the question, 'What is the best corrective?' Dealing honestly with oneself and shirking no issue, the conclusion may be reached that another earthly life is the best way to overcome that fault. The guides we have will then help choose the parents for us (yes, we choice our parents!) and the body to inhabit with the requisite inherited tendencies that will bring conditions suitable for the requisite training.

To find the perfect pair of parents is rare, so the next best is to find parents who will be mindful of the personal characteristics of their child and give it the parental care and education to bring out and develop its potential faculties. This is one of the hardest problems the guide must face when choosing the parents, for if the latter fail in bringing up the child wisely, as fail they sometimes do, then the child can grow up in discord and 'out of place'.

Reincarnation is a fact and is a voluntary act on the part of the returning spirit, but in the case of the 'low' degraded spirits, it may appear to have some compelling force behind it. Spirits that are very evil and have descended on to lower realms in spirit, can remain there for a very long time, even centuries. However, always there comes that moment when the first glimmering of a hope of the possibility of escape from that realm arises. These evil souls remain on a level that is like themselves. For example, the man that kills people for fun and was evil on Earth will stay with his own kind in lower realms in spirit. They will be given the chance to change and learn how to regain light, but they have to be willing to accept that.

The guide of each soul has never lost contact with his charge, even in the lower realm. The guide will not wish to remain in that realm, but he can make contact with that person with projected thought. At the first cry for help from the evil soul, help is sent out. The cry does not need to be vocal but may go out as a thought and a desire to progress. The guides would not be visible in the lower realms because of their advanced state. The evil soul can then be guided by its guide to try and go back to the Earth to reincarnate into a body and start its journey to progress.

Every soul wants to progress to a higher level, and that is why sometimes they wish to reincarnate. I asked Leazare a question that had always puzzled me. If our loved ones in Spirit reincarnate, then how will they come back to us on Earth? Leazare smiled and told me that again this was to do with time. In spirit there is no time, and so to us it may seem years until they wish to reincarnate, but to them it may only be a day. He also told me that the soul is energy and that again this energy can't be contained. It is free-moving just like any form of energy. It is not of a body anymore and so can be in many places at once.

My glimpse of a past life came from the site of a helicopter crash. I was told by Leazare that I have had many lives and that I was a soul that wished to come back to Earth to help others and shine light on the planet. He told me that the Great White Spirit would always be close by me and that I had now a duty to help others since I had chosen to return to Earth.

In my last life I was a helicopter pilot called Peter. I was in my mid-forties when I died, and I had been flying for most of my life. I was about to go out on a rescue mission with the helicopter above the Ocean in the USA. I was with a co-pilot, and we were talking away, when one of the blades of the helicopter stuck. I looked up above me and looked at my co-pilot beside me, and with that the helicopter blew up. There must have been a fault with it, and my last memory was hot burning fuel on my face, and then I was in my spirit body.

After this life, I chose to return to Earth to serve others. When I was a little girl, I had always loved helicopters! I would jump with joy at the sight of them, yet almost nearly every night I would dream I was flying in a helicopter, but then it would crash. Now I knew why I had this dream. My mum would hold me and tell me that she sensed I had been a pilot and that this was my soul remembering its last time on Earth in that body. She used to tell me that over time this dream would fade, and it did. Sometimes I do still have this dream, but now I know the reason why.

Chapter Eight:
Suicide and the Soul

This time my journey to the Spirit World was because I had tried to take my own life, so I asked my grandfather about suicide and the soul. He told me that he knew someone who held a better understanding and who would help me learn about this, and with that I found myself with my spirit guide Leazare.

Leazare told me that he loved me dearly and could understood why I had wanted to return to Spirit, but he also told me that I still had work to do. My wisdom and time should be used to help others who needed that help and understanding. He said that he would tell me all about the soul that tries to come to Spirit before their rightful time and what happens to that soul. I sat with him in the castle that I knew from a previous life, while Leazare looked at me with the same love and care that he always held for me.

Leazare said that there is much misunderstanding and ignorance concerning suicide and what happens to those who end their lives prematurely. The passing of a suicide and the awakening into spirit do not differ from those of one who passes unexpectedly by an accident, but the subsequent experiences differ because the mental conditions of the two spirits are not similar.

He said that it is absolutely incorrect to hold the idea that there is a special region in the Spirit World set aside for suicides; nor is there any power that compels such a spirit to undergo a particular punishment, such as remaining close to the Earth until the normal span of his mortal life is completed.

Leazare said that one who passed into spirit life by an accident may be very troubled in mind because he has left conditions behind that will make life very hard and complicated for a loved one. He will naturally do all that is possible to ease those conditions by impressing the mind of the one on Earth with the best action to take or the best words to say. In other respects the spirit is ready to experience all that this new life may hold for him.

There is a difference between this situation and the after-passing of the suicide. Not only is he concerned with the excessive sorrow and suffering he has inflicted on those he has left behind by this action, but he is also vitally concerned with the moral weakness in his or her character that led to this act. This weakness is a human fault, and when he is fully awakened to this fact, then that soul will need all the strength of character to purge it away. This is not done quickly, nor is mere repentance sufficient. Like any soul that has weakness, this spirit is helped and given advice and guidance by their guides and loved ones.

The soul that takes its own life has suffered, Leazare told me, much as I had. He told me that had I not been meant to return to Earth to do work for spirit but had instead stayed in Spirit, I would have been given much healing and help from all those that loved me. He told me that someone who takes their life is treated the same in spirit and is still loved and adored by all. The soul needs help and healing and will be given that healing just like any soul.

All souls that enter Spirit are unique with their own special unique lessons to learn. No one soul that commits suicide is the same as another soul that enters spirit. They all have their own weakness and their own learning to do.

Leazare told me that I was loved very much and that I must use this time in spirit to learn and grow so that I may go on to help others on Earth and show them that they all have a reason to live and a reason to have a good life and know that life never ends.

This again was another lesson for me from spirit to pass on to others, and this is what I am doing now. I was then ready to learn so much more while I was still in the Spirit World.

Chapter Nine:
Sleep and the Soul

I t is said that many people spend approximately a third of our lives in bed asleep; many of us sleep for around six or eight hours a day. Admitting this fact, then we may say that the spirit that is confined in the body must be active in some way whilst the body sleeps.

Sleep is an absolute necessity for the human. During our waking lives, much energy is used in one form or another, tiring the body. Although a certain amount of recharging takes place whilst we are still active, it is not possible to replenish fully until the body is quiet or asleep. During sleep the spirit beings, in whose charge we are, pour into our physical form that revitalising life and energy, strengthening it for the activities of the following day.

But the spirit isn't lying idle all this time. The soul-body of the spirit requires no recuperation, so this is the period of its release, when it can function freely apart from the physical body that has imprisoned it during the wakening hours. The spirit cannot be fully manifest when encased in flesh. The mind of the spirit is greater than the physical brain can portray, and its powers and abilities are hampered by the restrictions of the brain – hence those terms, the 'subconscious mind' and the 'superconscious mind'.

Many have said, 'I'll go to bed and sleep on it', with the hope of solving some problem they have. Why would this period of unconsciousness give a solution? Well, when the superconsciousness is freed from the restriction of the body, it is more capable of finding a solution than when it is submerged in the conditions that handicap it. Also, the spirit can talk to its loved ones

51

and ask for wisdom and advice. The soul may be capable of reaching a sound conclusion for itself when the mind is freed from the physical brain, for then it can use all its knowledge and experience in weighing the pros and cons. The superconscious mind holds all the knowledge belonging to the spirit, both of this life and of all the previous lives it has lived. The solution may then be impressed on the brain by the superconsciousness, via the subconsciousness, during the awakening, and yet it may come by way of a dream or it may come to normal consciousness as a thought.

Sleep overcomes the brain, and the spirit rises up and leaves its temporary body. It is free now to wander where it will during the period of coma; it can roam the Earth, travel in to the astral states, or enter in to a spiritual realm. The only restriction imposed is the spirit's development. None can enter a realm for which they are not fitted.

The spirit does not invariably wander away from its mortal body; it can rise above the body and remain there, freed from the limitation of the human brain, and spend the period in deep thought.

There are many who don't believe that we have a sleep life. This belief possibly arises from the same reason that they reject the theory of reincarnation: they cannot remember anything about it.

Once again memory is mercifully withheld, because it would unfit us for our dull working lives. Would we be satisfied with our lives and home conditions if we remembered where we had been or who we had been with? If we could remember this, would anyone be satisfied with their working life on Earth? No! We must live mentally balanced lives whilst on Earth, with no memories of better conditions to distract us from the satisfaction and enjoyment we can derive from our lesser pleasures.

It is possible to have an occasional memory come in the form of a dream. Many will relate wonderful dreams they have had – dreams that were outstanding compared to the usual type – and this experience of 'dreaming true' is the bringing back to the brain of a past experience that can be experienced as a dream. Many very spiritual people will give wonderful descriptions of vivid dreams or visions they have experienced during their sleep, and this is because their brains are so accustomed to being impressed for control, that it is a simple matter for an advanced spirit to impress on the mind a vision of some event that truly took place during sleep.

We can meet up with those people we love and care about during sleep. I am not just talking about those who have already passed on into the Spirit World. I am talking about those on Earth, even those that may live miles and miles from us.

It is amazing the amount of help we may give to others still living on Earth during that period of freedom. There is a wide scope for friends of all sorts who meet in the sleep state; some may have left Earth life behind, while others may still be on Earth, but the bond of love can draw them together. A mother's love can take her to her child anywhere on Earth. For example, if a mother has a grown-up son or daughter working in another country, the bond of love between them will take her to them while asleep, and she will see for herself how they are. On awakening, she may have a feeling that her son or daughter is ill. Well, this is because she knew already while with them in sleep. What we call intuition or a hunch is more frequently knowledge obtained during sleep, and the fact may be brought back as a dream or an intuition.

If it were only better known, then this sleep life would give great consolation to mourners. I would like to give an example of this.

A young mother had just lost her baby. She is a good Christian, and she fully believes that her child has gone to Jesus and will be cared for by a lovely angel mother. Her grief is based on the idea that before her time to die arrives, her little one will have grown into an angel, and she will never have her baby again and be able to hold it in her arms. Her grief can be intensified by another thought. Because her baby died before it was old enough to be conscious that it had a father or mother, when the time comes for them to pass over to spirit, they will be complete strangers to the child. How could it be otherwise? They too would not recognise their baby after all those years, and the baby never knew them. Those two ideas add an intolerable weight to the already heavy burden of the loss. The shame is that this reality does not exist!

The mother was correct in her belief that her baby would be cared for by a spirit mother, one of those women who dearly love children (like my gran). Under this care, the little one grows and learns. However, when the mother on Earth is asleep, she is in fact with her child. She sees it grow and learn, and she too is part of that care and teaching. She holds it and cares for it and is part of that little soul's life. When the time comes for her to return into her physical body, she goes with the knowledge given to her by the spirit mother that never again need she feel separation from her baby. Better still, the child will know its mother and grow in her companionship and love her as any affectionate child would do.

This is the same for all of the loved ones we have lost over to spirit, but some might ask why we should not remember being with them. Well, the comparison between being with them and then being apart from them would be too unsettling and cruel, and this is why we do not always remember that meeting.

Just as my gran had lost her little boy to sprit at such a young age, she too would have looked after him in her sleep life, and she would have seen him grow and would never be apart from him.

Leazare told me that we are always so close to those we love, and we are closer when we are in this sleep life that we all have.

Chapter Ten:
Prayer and Our Thoughts

Never a day passes without countless prayers being raised up to God and the Universe, asking for many things from forgiveness to a better job to better health for us or a loved one. Do we really have a proper understanding of what we are doing? Because of an ancient teaching of a God of Wrath, a God whom it is possible to anger, do we really know in our hearts who or what is listening to these prayers?

Many of us learnt as children to pray and to ask for what we need or want, but we also learnt that we must in return be good and do good things. As the child grows, this way of thinking may cause the child to lose the true meaning of prayer. Thus, they in turn feel that if they do not stay on a good path, they have no right in asking for anything. This way of thinking causes many to feel that they have no connection with prayer anymore. When such thoughts as these flood the mind, then it is easy to see why the power of prayer loses its hold, and the habit once broken is not always easy to get back.

I was told by Leazare that there is always a way to connect to the Great White Spirit, not only by the well-known way of prayer but by many other ways also. He told me that I would find a way of connecting with the Great White Spirit and use this always in my life.

In an ever-changing world it is not surprising that many people now find that the word 'prayer' has all too much to do with religion. This is the way I always found prayer to be. I was always told by my mum and gran that we need to pray to become closer to the Divine (God), but I found this all too much of a religion, and I wanted to find a way of connecting with the Great Universe without the need to bend on my knees and ask for what I needed.

Leazare sat with me during my time to the Spirit World and told me what prayer was all about and what the word really means. To pray, he told me, is not to supplicate God in any way, except for spiritual help and understanding. Prayer does not need words; it is a reaching out from the best within our being. Prayer is a devout desire to overcome and be freed from the bondage of the self, for the inner self to become master of the outer self. All hopes are prayers if they are sufficiently strong and from the heart.

It is right to pray for forgiveness if one has the understanding that such a prayer does not impute the Great White Spirit with anger at our misdeed; yet we do not need to ask forgiveness of the Great White Spirit, for nothing we could do can disturb that everlasting love that has all this understanding. We hold a wrong conception of the Great White Spirit if we believe we can offend him and then be received back into favour when we repent and ask for forgiveness. Nothing can stop the love the Great White Spirit holds for us!

When we send out thoughts in our mind that we are sorry for what we have done, we start a cycle off that causes us to want peace in our hearts for ourselves. This peace can help us to change the way we acted, and many people who are truly sorry for a wrong deed will try and change what they did or try and do things differently next time. It is known that some people may go to church and ask for forgiveness and not truly mean it, as they come back from the church and do the same thing again. Thought is the key to prayer. If we don't really feel it in our hearts and soul, then no amount of apologies will make that person really feel they have changed. Thought is what prayer is all about. Prayer grows beyond the fact that we should have a set time for prayer or a set rule about how to pray. We must use prayer which is thought at any hour of the day or night.

The Great White Spirit is love and wisdom and justice. Whatever happens to us is known to this spirit. The protection of someone we love does not rely on our supplications to him. When we implore God to save someone or protect them, we are actually reminding ourselves that there is a power beyond our puny, limited strength, and calling on this power is our comfort. Also, in our ardent prayer for another, we are releasing a subtle power for good; our thoughts are flowing out in unselfish love and in a way beyond our comprehension. This outpouring of power can be and is used by our spirit helpers.

Prayer is a constant communion by thought with the Spirit World, a companionship with the Great White Spirit that is more intimate than with an earthly parent. We should talk to the Great White Spirit at any moment without set phrases. An exclamation of gratitude to show that we can appreciate some beauty or nature or that a certain joy has been realised, little unpremeditated thoughts that arise frequently during each day given spontaneously to Spirit as we would to a parent on Earth – these are true prayers for they come from the heart.

Actions are the outcome of thought, and thought which considers others before the self is spirit predominating over the desire of the self. When we send our thoughts, our spirit is recognising responsibility and kinship to the eternal spirit, and this unconscious contact is prayer in its deepest sense. The real desires of our hearts, the desire we dwell upon in our minds and constantly strive to bring about – these are our true prayers, whether expressed or unexpressed.

We are all centres for receiving and giving out power. In order to receive, we must raise the level of our minds to the highest level we are capable. We must strive to tune in with the spiritual level, and then the power will flow freely from God and the Universe into our innermost spirit, and down into the consciousness.

After hearing this from Leazare and the Spirit World, I felt that when I was back to the earthly plane, I had a need to find a way of connecting to the Universe and Spirit without the need for all these words and ways of prayer. I now knew that prayer was thought and power that we send out to a higher place than this Earth.

I always used say my prayers day and night, and I also used to say them in a set way, without really thinking of what I was doing and why I was doing it. I now felt I wanted to change this, and so I started to talk to the Great White Spirit as a friend and not someone to fear and have to please.

I was finding this way with the Great White Spirit a much more personal and intimate way to feel that what I asked for I could receive. I also didn't feel the need to feel guilty anymore about what I asked for. I felt that if it was truly needed for the my own good and that of my earthly life, then all I had to do was send out a thought of what I needed and know in my heart that if I believed and knew it would happen, then it would come about. I felt that I was allowed to ask for things as well as thank God for things and that it was only natural that we can ask and know that we deserve to have good things happen.

This way of thinking was working, and the more I sent out thoughts and power and believed in them, then the more good things would happen. It was as if I had found a way to connect to the Great Universe and Spirit World. It was some years later that a dear friend told me that this way of thinking and of using prayer is called 'cosmic ordering'. This friend himself had found a new way of sending out thought to the Universe and to a higher power, and he had now spent much time writing on this subject and teaching it.

This is a New Age phenomenon. It is non-sectarian, non-religious, and in no way a cult. It is a new way for people to see that they can offer up their desires and needs and thoughts and to know that they are able to do this without the need for a set way of prayers or a religion to follow.

Cosmic ordering is all about this 'thought' that Leazare mentioned when he told me that I would find my own way for prayer that would feel right for me. I believe I found my own way through, and this is where I found cosmic ordering. Cosmic ordering is all about thought. We offer a thought in our hearts and minds of what it is we would want or what we need at a given time. Many people write this 'order' down on some paper, while others may say it aloud in their minds. When this is done, they have sent it out to the Great Universe as an order. The next key thing for this order to come about is to believe it will happen! Like a prayer that is said, we must hold on to it and believe that it is heard and will be answered. We need to believe that we are worthy of what we have asked for and that we can have this if we believe hard enough that it is working and that what we have sent out is a power that will bring about this new thing.

I was told by someone that cosmic ordering is like sending out an order in the post for an item. We consider what we need, and then we post the order off, be it by post or computer. We then know that we will get that order because we believe in it. It is the same with cosmic ordering or prayer. We ask for what we need or want, we post it in our thoughts, and we send out an energy and power. That energy is sent out and works.

But someone may say, 'Do I know it has worked or been heard?' I would reply that if you post a letter for an order on an item, you would not keep going to the post box to see if it had gone. Well, it's the same with what you ask for. You post it and send it out in thought and know that it will come about. You don't need to keep sending it.

I was once asked to explain cosmic ordering to a friend who had no idea what it was all about, and the following is the simple way that I explained it to her.

Cosmic ordering is all about the Universe and the natural energy around us all. We don't have to follow a religion to be able to ask for what we need or to express our gratitude. The cosmos and the planets are very much like us. They are not so different from the atoms in all of us, for there is a mini-universe in all of us. When we desire something, we are sending out a thought. For example, we may need a new job that would make us happier. When we think of this and think of the new job that would make us happier, we have then sent out a thought. This thought is energy, and energy can't be contained! It is moving around and around. The energy goes out into the Great Universe and is picked up by higher powers that are out there for us all (call them 'God' or just 'Universe'), and these powers begin to help this desire come about. If we doubt what we have sent out, then we are keeping that energy around us and not letting it go to where it will be worked on.

I always see it in this simple way, but it is a good way to explain how I see my cosmic orders answered. When we cosmic order or pray, we send out energy to the Great Universe. That energy lights up so many stars in the Universe! When the stars light up, they awaken the Great White Spirit. It is very much like an alarm clock. The Great White Spirit then sees that we have asked for something, and he will in turn send it back to us through the Universe in a parcel. We may not know when that parcel will come, as spirit has no time. Be sure though that it will come, because in the Spirit World we are dearly loved.

This was my very simple childlike way of explaining it to this friend, but this is what it is all about – being simple and knowing that no amount of words or having to do this or that will make Spirit or the Universe answer us. All we need is a childlike knowledge that it will come about, because we tuned in to that simple word, and that is 'thought'.

Chapter Eleven:
Why Some Souls Stay Close to the Earth

While I was taking in the beauty of the Spirit World, I remembered the second time that I had left the earthly body I was in and how I had felt such anger about the wrong done to me. My anger had become an energy that caused things in the room where my body lay to fly around and move and break. I wanted to know more about this and why this was so.

I was walking along a river bank as I was given more information about this next thing. My gran had come to join me and was telling me all about this as we walked arm in arm beside the river. This river was full of fish that I could see jumped from the water at every few steps we took. They were the biggest fish I have ever seen and they seemed to be in their thousands. The river looked again like a painting and the way it shone was like a box full of diamonds!

My gran told me that it had been my anger transformed into energy that had moved objects around in the room. This energy wanted a reaction, and the reaction was the moving object. She told me that passing over from this material world to the next is usually without trauma, because the soul recognises it has left the body and is still alive in spirit form. If the person went through a trauma and was killed by an accident or by someone else, then the spirit can be trapped between the two worlds and may refuse to leave the Earth realms where it lived. This is what people call a 'ghost'. This ghost will be similar in looks and attitude to the person it was on Earth. So if this person was angry and ignorant, then you can guess that his ghost will be too.

When I had passed from my body that first time, I was so angry and upset that if I had remained in Spirit form, then maybe I would have stayed close to the Earth and become a ghost. My anger might have caused things to move or make things happen to attract attention. Instead, I was taken by my loved ones to the Spirit World, and this is what happens to many souls when they pass quickly. Their loved ones will come to them and talk to them and tell them that they are now free and can go to the Spirit World in peace. If a person has no idea about spirit and another world or if they decide they are too angry to move on, just as a person on Earth may do, they may wish to stay there and not want to move until justice prevails. Their loved ones and guides can keep asking them, but they may still want justice and decide that they want to remain close to the Earth.

Our loved ones will never give up trying to help us and guide us, but like any of us on Earth, we may not always take the best advice from those that love us, and so we make mistakes and have to learn in our own time. In a similar way the soul that wants to remain close to the Earth may be waiting for justice and will not accept that justice may never come. Those souls may keep reliving that same trauma again and again, because their energy is keeping that trauma alive and they are so close to it that they keep living it.

Such a soul may stay close to a building or a person, and when someone that is spiritually aware enters the place, they may hear things or see things; this is because that soul is there thinking it is still part of that place. That place may keep changing year after year, but to that soul it is still the same place and nothing has changed. That is why some people, when they see these spirits, will say that they only saw the top half of the spirit and not the bottom half. That is because the place may have been built up, and that soul is still walking on the level that building was on Earth during its time there.

Some souls may at times see people from the Earth come to the place they stay close to and may hear that person talk to them. A good example is the 'Most Haunted' television show. When they say they are communicating with a person or persons, that soul has seen and heard them and may want the comfort of people. After all, they are just like us and want company. They may take the opportunity to talk to these people, because the people on that show do go there to find spirit. So if they are open to that, the spirit will know this and accept the invitation to join them and maybe gain comfort from them and their words. Some souls may need the comfort and understanding about what happened to them from the living, and when this is done they may then feel at peace to move on. This is what mediums call a 'spirit rescue'.

Some people may say that there is residual energy in a place. This means that the soul has left energy of itself there that can be felt or heard. It may not mean the soul is always in that one place; it may at times want to go to the Spirit World and meet its loved ones, but when it goes away, it still leaves behind the energy of what it went through and what it felt like. I have heard many people say that they went to a haunted place and could hear and see people talking and working away just as if they were still alive. There may be a number of spirits they can hear, just as some may hear voices from an old battle ground and hear the gun shots still. This doesn't always mean they are all there trapped in that place. It is usually energy from that great event, and just like a photograph taken of an action, this is a photograph being played of the past.

I asked my gran if the trapped soul is aware of the evil ones who have injured them, and she told me that because they remained close to Earth, they would still be able to see them, but they could not harm them. This would distress them even more, and seeing them would keep them close to the energy of the trauma, making it even more difficult for that soul to let go, but again that soul's loved ones would always try and protect them the best way they could.

Gran told me that ghosts and spirits inhabit the world around us all. We can hear and see them only if we are sensitive or psychic enough to be aware of them.

Some energies, she told me, may not always be good in a certain place. This is not always to do with spirit trapped on Earth. It may be a place that was used for evil and wrong-doing which has dark spirits there who wish to remain close to the Earth, either to commit more evil or through fear that they will be judged if they move on. There can also be bad energies that have remained in a building or place that will cause things to happen that may scare the living. Some people call these poltergeists (which means 'noisy spirits') or even demons. This may not always be the result of a very evil soul who stays close to the Earth, but can also be because that place has trapped bad energy. After all energy is living and can't be contained.

According to gran, there are such things as demons. These are not human souls, but they feed on evil and are another form of a bad energy that can collect in a place. She said that dark would attract dark and that this demon energy would and could use evil souls and influence them to do more evil. Some of them may influence rulers of places and try to cause a problem that would bring more evil to the world. It was also possible for these demon energies to try to use people on Earth who were already evil-minded and take them over to cause more harm to the world and its people. She told me that this was rare, because good spirits try to prevent this. It is not often heard of, but it was something that did happen.

My gran told me that there are times when our loved ones have not passed over but are poised between the Earth and Spirit. This can happen to people who are in comas. Some people wake from these comas and go on to talk of things they have done while in that coma just as if they had still been alive. Some even say they went home and watched television with their family. People may look and think this is crazy. But in fact this is real, as they have been with their loved ones and not trapped in the coma. The soul is free when the person is in the coma, and they are free like any other soul to move around and visit loved ones on Earth and in the Spirit World.

Gran told me that this was happening to me. She told me that my body had gone into some sort of short coma and that even though it wasn't long in Earth time, it would seem ages to me in Spirit. She told me that I was to learn from this trauma and that I would go back and remember everything that had happened to me while out of my body so that I could pass on the information to other people. Now I understood why this was all happening to me. I had learnt many things, such as what it was like for a soul that remained close to the Earth and wanted justice for its pain and terrible life.

Through these involuntary out-of-body experiences that are distinctly different from the most lucid of dreams, I was learning about our souls. It was evident to me that we are in essence spiritual beings inhabiting a physical body and that we can be temporarily released from the shell when we attain a deep state of relaxation during sleep, a coma, or under anaesthetic,

Chapter Twelve:
Love and Soul Mates

Love is the greatest gift to man. It is what many of us on Earth will always strive for from birth onwards. A baby will want the attention and love of its mother. It will not see the world and what it may not have but will want the love of its mother, and if it feels this love, nothing else will matter to that baby or even the young child. Many have said that children want love and nothing else. Some children may have every material thing in life they could want, but if there is no love and attention in their life, they will be very unhappy.

Love is the most precious gift life has to offer to us. It comes in many forms and levels of intensity. There are so many ways to show love. There is the love of a mother for her child, and then there is love for family members and friends, and then there is the sweet love of a relationship.

During my journey to the Spirit World, I did feel love of the highest form. This love is so hard for us to find while we are on Earth and in human form. This is unconditional love. It asks for nothing in return and only wants to love because it feels it. I felt this love while in spirit form, and I can tell you that it is the best feeling ever! I felt that I was loved and never judged and that I didn't have to act a certain way to get this love or be who I wasn't, but this love was always there and never went away. It was pure and special, and because I felt it, I knew that I too could be capable of it on my return to Earth.

I will never forget that feeling. It was just like the love that we all strive to get on Earth from those around us and those we meet. My gran told me while I was in spirit that love was God and love was what this Earth and Spirit are all about. She said that love can be misunderstood, and she told me that people fall in love with the idea of perfect love and not love itself. I asked her what this meant, and so she explained to me about love and its many forms.

My gran told me that because we are all human, we all carry faults and things that stop us being capable of giving unconditional love. She told me that the love of a mother is meant to be the purest, but if we asked everyone if their mother was like that, some might disagree and say that they never felt much love from their mother. Many mothers are capable of giving pure love and will want the best for their child and will do everything they can to stop that child getting hurt, but they too may not always show this unconditional love. She told me that many parents will love their child always, but sometimes the child may do something that upsets the parent, and then the parent gets angry and may withhold showing much affection. This doesn't mean that they don't love the child, but it shows that we all expect something in return for our love, be it good behaviour or being loved back the same way.

She told me that you will hear many people say, 'I don't show them much love because they don't show it to me.' This is what they feel love is all about – you love me or else I won't love you. She said that love is a deep feeling that couldn't be seen or measured. She told me that our true soul is made up of love and it is a gift we can all express and feel no matter who we are or how rich we are. We don't need an education to get it or a certain amount of money to buy it, for the saying 'money can't buy love' is true.

My gran told me that our loved ones in spirit love us more without condition when they pass over, because they see that love is not something they have to give to get in return. She said that the new soul sees the importance of this love and starts to learn how to give it unconditionally.

She told me that the love of our guides and helpers is also pure and unconditional and they see only love for us and want to care for us. She told me that even if a person doesn't realise that they have a spirit guide, the guide will still love them without condition. Now, how many of us can do that? How many of us can love someone with nothing in return? Not many, I would guess.

This is the pure love we would all love to feel on Earth.

My gran told me about soul mates and what this meant. She told me that my guide Leazare was a soul mate to me and always would be so. She said that soul mates did not have to be lovers but could be sisters or brothers or mothers or aunts, and so on. She said that many people will say, 'I would love to meet my soul mate,' and they will look for the ideal man or woman and think that they will find their soul mate in them. She told me that it was very rare for someone to meet their soul mate in a relationship, but that it was possible. There are so many demands that can be made in relationships that sometimes soul mates would find this a hard way to meet up.

I asked my gran to explain to me what a soul mate is. She sat me down by a bed of red roses and told me that soul mates are two spirits that have known each other in a life before. They may have had many lives together and may have suffered the same fate when on Earth. These souls may have been friends or lovers in another life, but it doesn't always mean that they will come back that way. They may come back as twins or meet each other much later in life as lovers.

My gran told me that people think that soul mates have to be in just one of our relationships on Earth, but this is not always true. She told me that we may have had so many lives and we were maybe very close to many people in each life, and so we may see them on our return to Earth and feel a link with them right away. She told me that many people will say when they meet for the first time, 'I am sure I have seen you before,' and this may well be true!

Gran explained that when two soul mates meet again, they will feel a love that fits right in with who they are and what they feel. Their relationship will feel just right. When in spirit, these souls have asked to be reborn again on Earth and asked to be very close again. Some may be so close that they return together as twins or brother and sister. They ask that they may have a life together and spend time on Earth together so that they may be with each other even if only for a short time. My gran said that twins may be born together who had been husband and wife in another life. They will not feel the same sexual feelings towards each other as they may have done on Earth in a former life, because it was all about love and unconditional love, and this doesn't mean sexual needs.

I asked my gran about love and sex, and she explained it to me. She told me that many humans mix up the feeling of love and lust. She told me that when a man and woman (or man and man, etc.) love each other, they take that relationship a step further and want to be so close and feel that love that they have sexual relations. This sexual relationship makes them feel bonded to each other and closer than ever before. Some men and women do not feel this bond and only feel lust for another and for their body. This is not true love-making, but was lust and just 'sex'. She told me that to be with a partner you love and to feel that love and connection is special and natural and will make each partner involved feel the love they share.

I asked my gran if I had met any of my soul mates while on Earth. She told me that my mother was one of my soul mates and that I would also meet the other one in a man. I wasn't shocked to hear that my mum was a soul mate, as we have always been very close and we shared a bond that nobody could or would dare break. I wanted to know more about this man, and she said that I would find him in time and would know him right away. When I looked into his eyes, I would sense a part of what we shared before. I didn't ask her anything else about this, as I knew that what she told me would one day come true.

My gran then took a rose from a nearby bush and gave it to me and said, 'love that will never let you go'. She hugged me and held me so tight that I felt I was the most loved soul there could be.

My gran's prediction that I would meet a soul mate in years to come did come true. I met a man who was part of my journey in getting well again after my trauma. I met him by chance, and when we saw each other we knew there was a soul connection. I saw in his eyes a love that didn't need words, and it felt as though I was back with my best friend. We had both suffered in life. I will never forget our first meeting; I am sure there was music in Heaven as we kissed for the first time. I felt a love for him that I had never thought possible. At that time his life wasn't perfect. He had suffered like me and couldn't always talk about it. We met when we could, and we both knew there were things keeping us apart and that every second we stole was magic. One night while we lay in bed, he held me so tightly that it was as if we were one with each other. When he awoke, he said to me that the night we had spent was like two nights in one! It was as though we had been in that bed for more than one night and we had held each other in a way that was so pure that I am sure Heaven played music to us both.

I knew in my heart that he needed to sort his life out in many ways before we could be together, and that night in bed I knew would be our last for a while. It was true that we never met again after that night. We had to part for many reasons.

Before we parted, he held me in is arms and said, 'Never forget that I love you, will you?' It was as if both of our souls knew we may not see each other again for a long time. I felt like it was me and Leazare all over again, and the feeling in my heart was so pure that I knew I had found the meaning of unconditional love on Earth. I didn't judge him or want in return. All I knew was that I loved him so much that we were part of each other. Words were not needed to speak that love. Even to this day I still feel it, and I hope he does too.

Many would say that I may never meet him again, but I feel that we will meet again and will share that love and passion we always had. I know that if it isn't on Earth I will meet him again in spirit, for souls that share that much love can never be parted.

I may later in life have new relationships, but I will always know that what we had was a soul-mate link and that he gave me the key to experiencing unconditional love . . .

Chapter Thirteen:
Learning to Cope with the Loss of Loved Ones

The pain we feel when someone close to us dies is a pain that isn't easy to explain. It is a pain that seems so hard to carry that we feel our hearts will explode with grief and sometimes anger at the sudden loss. It may be the loss of a parent or a child or a friend or even a pet we cared about, but the sting of death is still there.

While I was in the Spirit world, I was very privileged to see that my loved ones were alive and well and with me still. I could see that there was no such thing as death and that our fear for what that word can bring is the opposite of how we would feel if we realised that. There is no death and no end when we pass away. We live on! And we go to a place so amazing that it would seem that we have something to celebrate when we pass.

It is easy for me to say this because I have seen the Spirit World, and I know we go there and live on into another life. I know that there is no way that we die and that word 'death' through the ages may have caused so much fear, but it is not the end for our souls when we do pass on.

My gran sat talking to me yet again while I was in the Spirit World. She told me that when a loved one comes to Spirit they are welcomed by all those that love them, including their guides. It is like a celebration to them, while to us it is a loss. She told me that even those that know of a Spirit World still feel the same pain as anyone else, because after all it is a physical loss: we will not see them in the way we used to or talk with them or interact with them as we used to. It is only human to feel that pain just like anyone else. She told me that the greatest pain to man is the death of loved ones and that when we lose someone, it is a worse pain than if they were sick or ill. The fact that we may believe in a Spirit World or a Heaven doesn't take that pain or sting away, but if we knew there was more to this life, then of course it would help and ease some of our worry about such things as wondering whether we will ever see our loved one again or worrying whether our loved one is okay and safe and really happy.

If you look the word 'death' up in a dictionary, it will say that the word 'death' means 'end of life', 'extinction', or 'disappearance'. This is so untrue! There is no death, and my gran told me that such a word should never have come to the knowledge of man, for it was not a word that Spirit likes to use. There is a life, and 'end of life' does not happen; it is a new journey and a new start and a day that should bring hope and not pain.

My gran told me that humans who say they have no faith and have no reason to believe there is a better place when we pass away are the ones who are the most shocked when they pass over. She told me that most people will have some sort of idea that death is not the end. There are some people who cannot believe that we have a soul which continues on its journey, but there may be a small part of them that does wonder if they are correct that living on Earth in a physical form is all there is to experience. Somewhere they may even question themselves whether they are right in thinking we are just here and this is all there is.

You may even hear some people say, 'they live on in my heart.' This is true! If they live on in your heart and mind, how can they be dead? It wouldn't make sense. If you mean 'disappearance' and 'extinction' when you say 'dead', how can this be so if they still live on in your heart and mind? In fact, people who say there is no 'life after death' are usually people with a mind that likes to think and is scientific. So if they think about it, saying we die and that is it cannot be true. If we hold our loved ones in our mind and heart and there are always memories of them, that is energy, and energy can't die! It goes on, and if not in its same state, it will go on to another state. Surely the scientists should hold the greatest faith in 'life after death' as they are the ones that talk so much about energy.

I asked my gran what it was like when she passed to Spirit and what she saw when she got there. She told me to remember the dream that I had as a child when she passed away. She told me that this dream was true and was how she had come to Spirit. I was shocked and also happy as that dream had seemed so real.

When my Gran passed away, she was a good age and had lived a good life. Her physical body was ready to let go, and so, when I was still a child, she passed away at peace and with my mum by her bedside. I remember going to the care home she was in after I had come from school and seeing my gran at peace on that bed. She was still wearing the same smile she had always worn and she seemed to still be breathing. I held my mum's hand and found it hard to breathe as the sting of the passing took hold, and I was left feeling that my best friend had gone. I was aware she would be happy and still alive, but that didn't stop the pain in my heart and the lumps in my throat.

That night while I slept, I saw my gran on a ship. I was on a beach seeing this ship come in to shore. It had balloons on it and looked like it was about to come to land with a queen on board. To my shock it was a queen, but it was my gran! She came near the beach and took the final steps out of the ship into the water and onto the beach. I could see all people around her saying welcome and holding out their hands ready to hug her. Gran stood in her blue dress, singing along to a hymn that she used to love. I could see her looking bright and happy, and her legs that had failed her were now carrying her as if they were the legs of a young boy.

The scene was interrupted by my alarm ringing. Later that day, I told my mum about my dream. She said that gran believed that going to Spirit was like a ship coming in to loved ones. This is how my gran had said she would travel to the Spirit World when it was her time to leave. So this was how my dear gran had gone to Spirit, and this was how she had shown me she was okay that night as a little girl, by giving me a glimpse into her journey there.

My gran told me that people will come to Spirit the way their souls see it. Some may feel they are on a train, others may feel like they are flying, and some may even just feel they have been asleep and when they wake they are with their loved ones. It will happen any way that soul desires.

Death is a door to the next world and not an end. In the Tarot, some see the death card as a death or end, but in fact it is a good card and means a new start and a new journey and an end to the old. People in the past have even made up images of a man in a black gown coming to collect the dead, and they call him the Spirit of Death. This is man's mind making up what they think is right. To me it would scare anyone and is nothing more than a horror film and not the way our loved ones go to Spirit.

When we have to let go of a loved one, I know it is hard and is a pain that will only heal in time. People have their own way of coping with the passing and may do things that seem strange but feel right to them. Some people like to visit a grave and talk to their loved one, and this is fine, even though our loved ones are still with us and not in that grave. If this gives them comfort and gives them a connection to talk to them, then this is how it should be.

I always put flowers by the pictures of my loved ones that have passed to Spirit on special occasions like birthdays and Christmas, as I feel that they would rather be in the house with me than at a cold graveyard. I also like to spend time in my loved ones' favourite places, as I know they are there with me. My gran loved Blackpool in Lancashire, like most of my family, and many of my family members loved the ballroom in Blackpool Tower, and so this is where I go to feel close to them and to ask them for help. I always sit in the ballroom and see them dancing away to the music.

People will have their own way of coping. That is fine if it helps them to feel less pain, even if it seems strange to us. I always drive past a road where there is a tree that has flowers on it every day and little gifts at Christmas time. This is where a young man got killed on the road, and his family leave things on the tree where it happened. It makes me feel so sorry for the family, because I would love to run and tell them that their loved one is not by that tree, but he is with them in his favourite place. However, this is their way of coping and feeling that they are doing something for him, and if this helps them, then it can only be good for them.

There is no wrong and right way to mourn the loss of loved ones as there is no wrong or right way to pass to Spirit. We are all different, and at the end of the day that is what makes us all special.

I was very lucky to see the Spirit World and remember it all, but I still feel the pain of death and the sting it brings. I am still human and with human thinking, and like anyone else, the passing of a loved one leaves its mark on my life.

I have a few words written down that Spirit gave to me about the loss of a loved one. The words are:

I have been on this Earth as long as I need to now, and I want you to be happy for me. I have left the cell behind that my soul was trapped in, and like a prisoner set free from jail, I am now free from any pain and suffering. I am on a new journey to a great place. Like a person about to set off to a great place, I want you to wave me goodbye but know that I will be back. I will never leave you, for where there is love, there is no separation, and where there is a home for me, I will be back to visit. Your heart holds me near as I hold you near, and as you will not forget me, I will not forget you. I will come to you day and night, and I will make sure you are safe and happy. I will see you happy and I will be happy. I will see you sad and I will touch you and give you a hug. Things will change as time goes on but I know your love for me will never go as my love for you will never go. When you say my name, I will be there, and when you ask me something, I will do my best to answer it. I may not have the body to touch you as I once did, but I have the love in me for you that will be felt in your heart and soul. I will kiss you and you will think it was the breeze. I will hug you and you will think it was just a shudder. I will follow you and you may think it is just a shadow, but you will have my picture in your mind and that will always be my love.

When your time comes to be set free and come with me, I will be there. I will wait for you like a friend waiting for you to step off a train on a station, and I will take your hand and be eager to show you my new home. I will greet you the way I always did, and I will say these words to you that will awaken your soul to its new home and I will begin with the word 'Welcome'.

I hold on to those words, and when I read them, I always know that they are from the world of Spirit and were sent to me so that I may share them with you all.

Chapter Fourteen:
Animals in the Spirit World

When I was in the Spirit World, I was always in a place of nature, be it the sea or the countryside or a waterfall. Also, I was always surrounded by animals and most of my pets that I had known on Earth. So when I hear the question, 'Do our pets go to the Spirit World?' the answer is a big 'Yes'!

My animals would follow me in the Spirit World, and I would see them as if they were still young. Not one of them seemed to carry an ailment that they may have carried when they were in their last days on Earth. For example, as I have already mentioned, my tabby cat called Sam who lost his tail in a road accident had a long and fluffy tail in the Spirit World.

I even saw my goldfish that I had looked after as a child. When I was in the Spirit World and near a river, I could see them gliding along the current of water that was as clear as glass.

Animals are Spirit too! Over the years many people have asked mediums what happens to animals when they pass into Spirit. It would be easy to say that animals are Spirit like us. They live, they pass on, and they can come back again as we may do. In Spirit they experience very much the same type of growth as we humans do. They are able to return to Earth again and may even decide to come back in human form. Their soul is more advanced though, and because they have learnt much more than humans about the natural way of living and consciousness, they tend to come back again in animal form to show love and care to humans. Some come back to be close to a human they once loved who may still be alive.

Animals are much more aware of Spirit; they use their instincts to respond to their owners and to strangers. They are just as sensitive as a medium or anyone else who has allowed their spiritual side to develop. They are more likely than a human to be alerted by a sense that's outside the five conventional ones – seeing, hearing, smelling, touching, and tasting.

Leazare told me that many humans would find this answer distressing. After all, humans are supposed to hold a very special place within creation, and they do, but this does not mean that we humans are the only living spirits in the Great White Spirit's kingdom. He told me that animals are spirits, plants are spirits, and even rocks and minerals are spirits.

Leazare told me that animals were given to man to learn from and to receive love and friendship. He told me that every animal has a purpose and a reason to be on the Earth. He said that even creatures like wild rats have a reason and a spirit and will teach man something about life. Man can learn from the great creation, and if he could follow nature and its many wise ways, then he too would learn much wisdom. He told me that bees seem to be such small creatures, but look how they work together to produce fine honey and look how they know their job and what they must do to get this honey. They do not question it and doubt that the honey will be made. They work and have faith in what they do, and the end result is pure honey that is always perfect and sweet. The bee teaches us to always have faith and to be patient, and in return good things will happen and come to us. Nature works with the bee, because the bee works with nature. Leazare told me that if man could learn this lesson, many good things would come to him.

He told me that the Great White Spirit had given us animals also as friends and companions to love us and care for us. Thus it is with our beloved pets. They come into our lives and give us such joy and companionship. They are spirits and deserve to be loved and respected as such. Their love is totally unconditional, and they can show us this kind of love that many humans fail to do. Many people will have a pet as a friend, and this love and friendship is much stronger sometimes than that of man. Their love and care is never-changing, and if we have a falling out with them, they soon come back to us with the same love as if nothing had happened. How many humans can do that? Not many, I guess.

Animals do not communicate in exactly the same way as humans do, but their communication tends to be more thought-form oriented. They do not develop speech on Earth, yet they communicate with telepathic transmissions of thought-forms and desires. When a dog wants something, he will sit and stare intently. You can see he is focusing his thoughts and thinking so very strongly what he desires to communicate with the owner.

When animals pass to Spirit, they do have a voice box and they do speak! Many of my pets spoke to me with gentle voices. I never thought this was so until I heard it myself in the Spirit World. The strange thing was that it never shocked me as you would think it would. I guess that on Earth many of them used to have such strong telepathic transmissions that I must have heard their voice while on Earth too without realising this.

When animals we love pass to Spirit, they endeavour to link with us and let us know they are well and safe. Just like a child passes to Spirit before the mother and she cares for it in sleep, well, this is the same with the pet. We will still care for it while we are asleep, and so will our loved ones in Spirit.

Animals will come back to us with the same love and care that they had for us on Earth. Many people may smell their pet or feel that their leg has been touched, and it has, for this may be their pet rubbing against them!

I have heard many mediums give people messages from their lovely pets from Spirit, and their message comes forward in much the same way as if it were from a human. They appear through clairvoyance just as humans do. They give evidence of their survival by showing themselves as they were while on Earth and conveying many of their character traits. Communication from a pet can be just as moving as a communication from a human.

Our animals are so important to us, and I know that my animals have given me a new life and are in many ways my little children. They have given me such love and care, and without them I am sure I would have gone insane. They also showed me how to be patient and how to show love without condition. My animals from Spirit always come back to me now, and I often see them around the house or feel one of my spirit cats asleep on my feet at night.

Many people have had experiences of their animals returning to them after death. They bring comfort by showing that they are safe and free from pain and suffering now. Above all this they come back because they love us. This is a poem I wrote about pets in Spirit.

I am always your little friend and that will always be.

When I pass over to Spirit, you will still be close to me.

I am still your little fluffy friend,

And that will never end.
I will come back to see you,
And my body will be new.
I will show you I am still near,
I may rub against you, so don't fear.
When you are down and all is dark,
I will be near and by your heart.
And when your time comes and we are together,
Our love will always be forever.

Chapter Fifteen:
Why There Is Suffering in This Life

While I was in the Spirit World, many of my questions had been answered, but there was one left, and that was 'Why do we have to suffer so much on this Earth?'

In the time I was in the Spirit World, my earthly body was still being abused and harmed, and I wanted to know why this was allowed when I had seen such a beautiful world. I wanted to be part of that world and not an evil one where there was so much darkness.

Leazare had spoken to me a lot about spirits that were of a low form and how they had to progress, but I wanted to know things like, 'Why does a baby die before it is born?' and 'Why do people get cancer?' So I asked Leazare why people on Earth experience suffering. At the time he was standing near a beautiful waterfall that was far more stunning than the ones you see on television or abroad in a far-off land. This was one that took on a shine like pure gold and contained pure water. Its water was so pure that no painting by the hand of a man could imitate this scene. If I could have drawn this picture, I would have loved to do so to capture this lovely image, but unfortunately my art skills go no further than stick people! I sat down by this waterfall with some of my spirit pets around me, and I was given an insight into the many reasons for the pain we all feel on this Earth plane.

Leazare spoke to me about the pain on the Earth and told me that many of the problems today were caused by the hand of man himself. He told me that the Great White Spirit had no intention of causing anyone pain and that we all live a life surrounded by the love of Spirit, but that to experience the purpose for which we came to Earth, we have to feel the pains of a human life and the hurts of this life in order to grow. He gave me an example of the child that is born and passes to Spirit quickly before he or she has even taken a first breath. He told me that the soul of that child decided to be born for that short time to the Earth just to experience the feeling of being wanted by a mother. He told me that this soul was given to the mother for that short time so that it may feel the life of being wanted and cared for and that being inside the womb of the mother, it would experience this care and then feel ready to return to the Spirit World. As I told you earlier in this book, every baby that passes to Spirit is still cared for by the Earth mother while they sleep, and the child grows and develops as it would have done on Earth. Sometimes the child may even pass when it is still very young, and this is because the soul needed to experience being a child on this Earth and learning as a child before it made its journey back to the Spirit World.

Children are such innocent souls and they are truly a gift from Spirit to us. While they are with us on Earth, it is our responsibility to love, nurture, guide, and remind them of what is good in life, but they are spirits as well as physical, mental, and emotional beings, and they too have to experience life like any of us adults do. It may seem hard to think that this child should suffer and feel pain, but this soul is here like all of us to learn and progress on its path. Parents are there for the child on Earth and are there even if the child passes to Spirit. However, the child is still its own little soul on its journey in life, and that soul has no responsibility to be bound to the Earth as it passes on to the next stage.

This brings me on to the subject of abortion. There will always be arguments for and against abortion on Earth. While I was talking to Leazare, this is something he talked to me about. Leazare said that we are not our physical bodies, but the spiritual being which animates us. The spiritual us never dies. From the moment of conception, a soul who has chosen to link with those parents will connect with that event with foreknowledge of what the outcome will be, whether a normal birth or a cessation for some reason.

That foreknowledge means that when a baby is to be aborted or there is a natural ending to the pregnancy, the soul involved will only experience life for that brief period in order to gain necessary understanding. There are no accidents in that sense, and no child is ever lost.

No one can judge why a woman decides to do this. It's an incredibly personal, private reason, religious for some and even connected with medical problems. In most instances, an abortion is not something a woman enters into lightly. It is a tremendously hard decision to make, and some women carry a burden of guilt about it for the rest of their lives. Spirit understands these feelings and works with the woman while she is going through this decision.

When babies die physically (whether in the womb or after birth), they pass to Spirit and then grow up in the normal way, cared for either by loved ones already in Spirit or by special loving individuals who perhaps didn't have the experience on Earth. If there is an instinctive sense of love from the natural mother and she wants to still care for this baby, then this is possible and she will do so like any mother who has lost her baby. She will care for the child while she is in sleep state and see it grow. Some women conceive through rape, and this is something that Spirit knows is already hard to deal with without the burden of having to carry that child. The woman is never judged, and the spirit of that unborn child will grow in Spirit with parents that never had the chance to care for a child on Earth. The natural mother does not need to have any connection with this child unless it is her instinct to want to care for it while she is in sleep state. This child is a spirit that is individual like any other spirit child, and just because it was conceived through violence does not mean that its soul carries the same karma as the one who committed the rape.

As with any deed done on Earth, it is only humans who judge themselves. If a woman knows in her heart that she couldn't give birth to that child for whatever reason, then it was right for her and the unborn child at that time. If she feels guilt, this is something she has to work through with the love and help of Spirit. People on Earth judge each other, but Spirit and the Great White Spirit never judge us or our actions.

No human escapes pain on the Earth. We all get sick and are open to catch disease while we inhabit a human form. Every soul comes to the Earth with a purpose and a new lesson they wish to learn. It is so hard, Leazare told me, to think that any child should suffer at all while on the Earth. Many people have blamed God when a child dies young or has a disease which causes the child to have pain and suffering.

I told Leazare that I agreed that all pain was wrong, and he told me that if there were no pain and suffering, then every soul would remain stuck to the Earth forever, because it had not developed in its stages and experienced things. He went on to explain that to experience something, we have to feel it. He said that it is like someone tasting a certain food. It is difficult for them to explain to another person what they have experienced.

The person needs to try it for themselves. We all have to experience things to know what they are like and how to develop from them.

He told me that people born with blindness or other health problems and disabilities would have asked to go through that way of life in order to experience certain things for progression of the soul. He told me that the soul that comes to the Earth blind may be born that way in order to see more of what is important. Leazare told me that some souls like this are able to see more than someone with eyes, because they open up other senses and see more than the man with eyes. They rely on feeling more and sensing what is around them, not just a physical feeling of things but a knowing of what someone looks like or a picture in their mind of what a place is like. This soul is learning about things that the man with eyes may never learn.

A person born without the ability to use their body may have chosen this life so that they can learn to be still and learn wisdom that no person with legs or arms may learn. They learn to use parts of their brain to help them in ways that a walking person may not have.

All this would be hard to take in, said Leazare, as man sees no reason to have such illness, and many say that no one should suffer, but he told me that Earth is like a school. It is hard and full of lessons. No one has to be born to Earth unless they want to be. They have free will and have chosen this life to develop their soul for progression.

Leazare told me that many of the diseases of the world today were brought about by the hand of man and that man was responsible for how the Earth was changing and the illnesses now growing in the body of man. He told me that man used to live by nature and that in nature man would find a cure for all illness, if only he went back to the roots of the Earth and wouldn't try to find the answer in the evil he does to living animals. He told me that this was where man was going wrong and that the illness of today was getting worse because man is moving away more and more from the natural healing found on the Earth itself in plants and herbs.

He also told me that this was part of man having to learn about responsibility. We must learn how to live a life that can show us that we have been given this planet to care for and look after for all of us living this earthly life. If we abuse it and misuse it, then it will not take care of us and give us the best. Instead we will have disease and disasters.

I asked Leazare the question of why we should all suffer if certain men harm the world. He gave me an example. He told me that the world was like a great household for all souls to learn and develop, like a family.

There may be someone in that family that acts a certain way, for example, the man who drinks a lot so that there is no money in the family pot, and the whole of the household goes hungry because he spent the money on alcohol. Just like in a household where one family member is doing something that affects all the family members, one evil person can cause many problems. It may seem unfair, but if all the family did not suffer from what that person was doing to the household, then no lesson could or would be learnt, and that family member would be free to go on and do more and more things with no consequence.

The Earth is for us all to care for, and Leazare told me and that if we cared for it, the Earth would look after us in return. We live on a beautiful and amazing planet. We only have to look out to the sea to see what an incredible world we inhabit. All of us can enjoy this beauty as our birth right if we look after the planet and its creatures.

I was starting to understand why we all have pain and illness, but I wanted to know more about good and evil on the Earth and why good people have to suffer the pain from those that are evil. Leazare explained to me all of this.

Goodness and badness are opposite sides of the human personality, yet the thoughts we have on good and bad are not fixed, unchangeable points of cosmic law. The life we live on Earth is subject to many rules of the country or land we live in, and the human follows those laws like anyone else. There are rules that formulate our thoughts. Years ago, to burn someone at the stake for a silly crime was thought to be normal and right. Today, we would consider the one doing the burning evil and not the person who had done the 'crime'.

Each person has values subject to the socialisation process they have experienced within their lives on Earth. What constitutes crime and evil shifts through the ages. Humans say that a man who goes to war for his country and kills is given a medal for bravery, but if they killed someone in the absence of war, they would be put in prison and would be called an evil person.

Leazare told me that we are all learning more and more through each lifetime, and we are slowly evolving towards the light of the Great White Spirit's love. He told me that if we did not know what was evil, bad, and wrong, then we would never be able to recognise good. He explained that we all have the power to act well or badly, and if we know in our heart that what we are about to do is wrong and it feels wrong, then we are experiencing the real power of the Universe, and that power is telling us that what we are going to do is in fact bad. If we know that what we are going to do is good, and it feels right even though some may see it as wrong, then we are acting in a way that is right and with good intention.

Leazare said that any evil deed will not go without a karmic debt. This must be repaid, and there is no escape. Time may pass, and that soul may have to live many lives before it repays that debt, but it will have to pay it and learn from it in order to move on in its soul progression.

Many souls that do terrible things to people or animals on Earth may not be ready to face this karma until they are ready to progress and want to learn from their wrong, as Leazare spoke of before. Some souls may be so dark that they may have to stay on lower planes until they are ready to progress. These souls may have to wait for a long time until they repay the karma they collected from their evil, but in a lifetime they will repay it! Sometimes we do small things that do harm other people, and many of us will find we pay for this within a short time. An example I was told would be a person that has bullied someone at school or work, and later finds that they too are a victim of feeling trapped or bullied by someone. It may not come directly from another person; it could be that they are trapped in a lift for hours on end so that they know the feeling of being alone and what that feeling of being trapped felt like for their victim.

Leazare told me that there are many evil souls that kill and harm others for fun and pleasure and that these souls are the lowest there can be. When they are on Earth, they will attract people like themselves, and they seem to carry energy with them that even the person who is not spiritually aware may pick up on. They are souls that are a beacon for dark, and Leazare explained that the people that had done the wrong to me on the Earth always seem to collect in groups. As the old saying goes, 'Like attracts like.' He said that these souls may want to progress while still in this life and may see the error of their ways and change, but some are so dark that it takes so many lifetimes for them to even want to progress.

He told me that many people who have been the victims of these evil ones worry that when they pass on to Spirit, they will meet with them again. This is untrue, for, as Leazare told me before, these souls are on a lower level and stay there until they are ready to want to progress. Some may never want to progress, and it may take what seems like eternity for them to have any intention of wanting to progress. However, those that do want to progress may feel that they want to say sorry to their victim for what they did. That soul (who was the victim) is then asked by their guides if they would like to meet this other soul so that they may talk to them and say their piece, but if that soul doesn't want to see them, they have a right not to, and so their guides will pass the message on for them.

Leazare told me that he hears many people on Earth say, 'But the bad people always get on better and have more money and better health!' He told me that this may be true. They may have more money and better health, but money is grounded and will not pay for your soul to be closer to the Great White Spirit. We can all ask to come back to Earth and have more money if we like, but the soul will progress and see that money is only what is needed on Earth, not for the soul. Another example is the evil one with better health. They may be well on this Earth, but when they pass to Spirit, they still have to progress and learn, and they will stay on the lower levels until they do. The soul that suffers and may not have a great life may be the soul that is far more progressed. When those people pass over, they see beauty and spiritual wealth that no rich man on Earth will see.

I was so excited by all that Leazare had told me about the pain and evil in the world that I wanted to run and tell everyone what I had learnt. It also made me feel less bitter towards those that were doing wrong to me. I knew that if I let them truly win, I would have to sink my soul to their level and act as they would. I would have to hate and be bitter and act with violence like them, and then they would truly win, as their soul would bring me down to their level. I knew I was better and more advanced than that, and so I knew I had to make sure I carried on living a good life and being a 'light worker' and not let them take my soul. I always used to say to those that hurt me, 'Take my body and use it! Take my mind and play with it! But you can never take the soul from me!' Those words are true, and I always follow what Leazare told me just before I left this waterfall: 'We are Spirit first and we are body last.'

Chapter Sixteen:
The Journey Will Never End!

I guess many who have read what I have said so far will wonder whether I was in some sort of dream state, and to that I would answer, 'Yes, maybe I was, but that dream state must have been a very powerful one for me to be given many of life's answers to what will happen to us when we pass on in life. I believe that for me to be given so much detail was much more than a dream!'

Some may even wonder whether I am insane! To this I answer, 'Well, I will answer that one when you yourself are ready to pass to the World of Spirit. Then you may come back and tell me that I am insane!' I also laugh, because some may very well still come back in their spirit form and tell me I am insane. After all, when we pass over to Spirit, we are still the same people with the same personalities.

I have always been a spiritual person, and so I guess that is why Spirit found it easy to work with me. Had all my pain and suffering been for nothing, then I may well have felt a victim for the rest of my life, but that is not to say that I did not still feel a victim for many years. Even though I knew that what I had experienced was very special, it still took me a good many years to realise that what I had been given was for others to know and not just for me to keep to myself in my victim's world.

Years after this experience, I would talk to my mother about it all, and I would tell her that I wanted to be with Spirit so badly because I felt that this Earth was too dark for me to stay on. I wanted to be with my loved ones, and I did on a number of occasions try to take my own life to get back what I had felt when I was in Spirit. I guess this was the risk Spirit had taken in giving me so much information and showing me so much, but now I know that it was a risk that did pay off, as it has helped me to write about my experience and also to share my gifts and the gifts of Spirit with people.

My life after my trauma was one of a lot of pain and suffering. It was not all a bed of roses after this lovely experience, and the one that helped me stay alive and be here to tell the tale was my dear mother with her love and the love of Spirit. I would spend many hours crying and wanting to know why it was that I was feeling so depressed. No tablet could help heal the pain I was feeling, and I would hit such a rock bottom that I look back now and wonder how I did manage to stay alive. I can now answer that one. It was because I was surrounded by the love of Spirit, and they did all they could to keep me here on Earth so that I may be able to help others with my gifts.

I had many experiences after my 'walk on the other side', and I would like to share some of them with you. After this great experience, I had many occasions in dream state where I would be back with my loved ones and be talking to them. When I was asleep, I would be given a lot of love and comfort from my family in Spirit. They would be as real as if I were awake, and I knew that I had been with them, because they would tell me things about the future and what was going to happen that always came true. I would feel as if I had gone home to my true family, and when I awoke I found that I would feel a lot better and be able to cope with the day.

There were also many occasions when they would leave things for me – things from Spirit called 'apports'. An apport is a physical object brought through Spirit to communicate with us. It may be almost anything – flowers, books, jewellery, and even coins. I was on one occasion given an old coin from them that I still have now. It dates back to the 1800s, and I remember finding it by my bedside one morning when I woke up and had just had a dream that my gran had been giving me some change from her purse. She told me she wanted to help me all she could, and when I awoke and found the coin on the floor – well, you can imagine the shock! I became very emotional and ran to tell my mother about it all.

Mother was not shocked. She told me that when my gran was a little girl, she didn't always have a lot of money, and so at Christmas she was never given a great deal. This never worried my gran, because the love of her family was all she cared about. One Christmas, my gran said she was sitting by the log fire, when she heard a bang within the fire place! She ran over to it and found a glass hopscotch. (This was a disk used for a game in my gran's days). Well, you can imagine the smile my gran had! She said that it was only very well-off kids that had such a gift in those days. She told my mother that she had kept that gift from Spirit for years and that she was the envy of the other kids in their road. She said that she knew it was from a special place, but back then she thought Father Christmas had sent it down the chimney.

I had many experiences. Some of them were so profound that I even had to sit and get my breath back afterwards. On one occasion I was sitting watching television, and what looked like a white rose flew across the room. My mum looked at me in shock and asked me who had just done that (thinking it was me or my father). When she said those words, we both heard a man's voice say, 'Me, your dad'. My mum knew that this was her father from Spirit, and he had not only been able to send an apport, but he had also been able to communicate directly to us all in the room.

This was not the only experience. We would often hear a piano playing from nowhere in the house, and after we had all searched the rooms to find this piano sound, we all came to the conclusion it was from the Spirit World. I guess that these experiences seemed to get stronger and stronger, and it was as though the Spirit World was only a foot away from us all. I feel that because I had been able to travel to the Spirit World, I had indeed brought back a lot of their energy and love, and this stayed with me even in my normal everyday life.

This was not the only sort of experience that I was having. I found that my psychic abilities were getting stronger and stronger, and even when I was out and about in my daily life, I was able to sense many things from people around me. It was as though I could see into their minds and see what they were thinking and feeling. I was able to sense what was going on around them in their lives there and then, and I was sensing what was going to happen to them. Of course, this was not something I wished to share with complete strangers in the street, and so I had to go home and meditate for hours and ask Spirit to help me contain this energy and use it when I was able to for the good of all.

I was able to give family members accurate messages from the Spirit World and I was able to speak to Spirit as if they were in the room and living with us. I had always been psychic, but this ability was getting stronger and stronger, and I was able to make predictions for myself and my friends, and these things always happened without fail.

I wanted to take this a lot further, and so I asked my mum what would be the best way to work for Spirit and use this energy for the good of all. She spoke to me at length and told me that I should use these gifts to help as many people on Earth and in the Spirit World as I could. She directed me to work from some of the Spiritualist churches and so this is where I started my work.

I remember the first time I stood on the church platform at the Spiritualist church. I was so scared to be facing so many people. I remember saying a few words to Spirit before I started and asking them to help me with their love and strength and asking them to assist me in helping these people have a small glimpse into the World of Spirit.

I started a connection with a lady who had just taken a seat in the church. She looked so tired. It seemed that she had been rushing about and had just made the service in time. I saw with her a lovely light, and this light turned into the figure of a lady that seemed very close to her. She was comforting this lady and wanting her to know that she was with her. I started to tell this lady what I had seen, including a description of the lady who wanted to show her love to her. She started to cry at what I was saying and told me that the lady I could see was her mother. She was shocked as I went on to describe this lady more and more, and I gave her a message from her mother. The message opened up more and more, and it was as if I was back in the Spirit World again and they were more real to me than those on Earth.

I went on to give message after message, and the look on people's faces was of amazement, for I am sure many of them thought I was too young to be a medium. I was happy that Spirit had come through so strongly that I was able to see them and hear them and pass on to their loved ones such comfort and joy.

I found that after this I wanted to do more and more work for Spirit. I continued doing more services with my mum at the churches, and I also went on to work at a small New Age shop in my home town of Dudley. I found that the link I had with Spirit was very strong, and I felt that sometimes in a church environment I wasn't able to open up the message as much as I would have liked because of human rules and regulations at the churches. So I found that I wanted to use this energy and link with Spirit in other ways, and that is why I started to study things like the tarot cards and the crystal ball.

I first learnt the tarot cards from a lovely friend who had worked with them for years and also taught people about them, and so I was lucky to have private lessons from her and learn them for myself. I used them in my readings and messages from Spirit to help give people a link and a feeling that there was something there for them to see – not just me looking into empty space. This seems natural to me, but for some people I found that the Tarot or the crystal ball gave them a feeling of something real and something they could understand.

I always found the crystal ball so much better to use, because I only used the Tarot and crystal ball as tools and a link to Spirit. Spirit could come through in many ways and didn't need an earthly object to be able to communicate. I could hold the crystal ball and see Spirit through it as clear as if I were looking through a mirror.

I worked at the shop for a few years, and my reputation was growing and becoming well known around the area. I was asked to help many people who had lost loved ones, and I would do my best to help them and invite them to my home so that I could link to their loved one in Spirit.

I never charged people, as I felt that this gift was so natural and that I needed to help people and let them have that time with their loved one. I used to tell people to give any donation they could afford to a charity, as that way they would be showing respect for the messages and giving back to the goodness of the Earth. I felt that if I did this, they would use the message I had given them for good and appreciate the effort Spirit had made in coming through to them, for it is part of human nature that if we receive everything free, we do not always appreciate what we have been given. That is why I always asked that a donation be given to a charity.

It was not just my messages from Spirit that developed more and more, but I also found that I wanted to use my healing gifts to help people and animals. I wanted to again use this healing in a natural way and not let it be contained in any church, and so I found out about Reiki healing. I had on many occasions received Reiki myself from the New Age shop and from a lovely gentleman there that used to give people healing. I found that it was helping me so much, and I would return often to receive more.

I wanted to learn Reiki for myself, and so I found a lady in the area that was teaching it. She was an American lady who had married an English man and lived with him in England, where she was teaching Reiki and helping people understand more about it. We became friends as soon as we met, and from that day on we became like sisters, and I am sure we both had a spiritual link where we were meant to meet in life like this.

Reiki is a natural healing art whose name translates as 'universal life-force energy' and involves the act known as laying-on of hands to heal a person or animal. What separates Reiki from other methods of hands-on healing is the manner in which the ability is passed on. When new healers receive energy from the teacher or master, they develop the ability to heal themselves and others. Next they can receive the potential to become masters and pass on these skills to others as I have. Many believe that we all have the ability to heal others. With Reiki this function has been restored through a realignment of the life-force energy. The Ki or Rei-ki is the Japanese name for this energy. In Chinese it is Chi, and Indians know it as Prana. This force is essential to a living organism; it is the life force of all living things.

Reiki practitioners believe that not all medical problems are physical only; some are based in emotional and mental disorders whose source might be difficult to discover. This was true of many things in my life, and my physical problems did have an emotional attachment most of the time, and I could see that Reiki was showing this to me.

The primary purpose of Reiki is to allow the healer to become a channel for the energy known as Ki. As a Reiki practitioner, I am only a channel for this energy. My personal energy is unaffected by a session of healing. Reiki is the opening of this universal energy to come through and help the person or animal.

The history of Reiki is in some parts clearly documented, but it is always dependent on the opinions and point of view of the historian of each particular text. This following account is the main history taught to people who learn Reiki.

Dr Mikao Usui founded Reiki at the end of the nineteenth century. Usui was then the director and Christian minister at the Doshisha University in Kyoto, Japan. While reading to his students about the miracles of Christ, Usui was asked whether his own belief in Christ's ministry meant that he could imitate these miracles. It is said that this question was what sent Usui on his quest for more knowledge about this healing.

After applying for direction to the Christian authorities in Japan, he was informed that such healing was neither practised nor spoken of in the Catholic Church. He then travelled to America, where he received a doctorate in theology, and among other skills learnt to read Sanskrit, the ancient language of India.

He recognised the similarities in the life of Buddha and Christ, both of whom were able to heal at touch, as well as from great distance. He widened his search to include ancient Buddhist texts and finally came upon the mantras and symbols which were the code for what is now Usui Reiki.

Usui spent much time in a Buddhist monastery and, after explaining his difficulty to his spiritual teacher, was advised to meditate while fasting. He did this for twenty-one days on a mountain in Japan called Koriyama. Just before dawn on the final day, a great light struck him in the middle of the forehead. The experience that followed was a spiritual one. He described a mass of brightly coloured bubbles. They settled to form the symbols from the tantra lotus sutra. Along with his conscious knowledge of how to use this spiritual power, he was endowed with the healing force itself.

Reiki became a great part of my life. I started out mainly helping my animal friends and horses at the local stables. I would give healing to as many animals as I could, and in return I saw many of them get well and recover fully. I remember in particular one horse called Sunset. The owner of the stables had owned this horse for a number of years. He was very old and ready to pass to the Spirit World, but he was suffering, and his physical body wouldn't give in the fight. The owner didn't want him to have to be put to sleep because the way this is done for a horse is not too pleasant. I spent hours with Sunset, giving him Reiki and energy, and after a few days I received a call to tell me that he had made his transition to Spirit peacefully in the night. I was happy and grateful for the owner and Sunset, and I thanked the Great Universe and its energy and Spirit for this.

After my experience in the Spirit World I also found that I had a natural empathy with people and suffering. I became very sensitive to the needs of others, and I would feel great pain for them and the suffering of the world. I knew that I had to be careful not to drain myself this way by feeling so much for others and forgetting my own needs. I was told that I could use this empathy while doing counselling and in the training they would teach me how to control my own personal feelings around these people.

So I started many training courses in counselling and mental health issues. On the counselling courses, I was always the one who would exceed in the work, and I was told by two of my tutors that I had a 'natural flair of sensitivity' in how I worked with people. I was also asked to help the other students in their work, and I found that I had a natural gift and love to do counselling work.

To complete my counselling diploma, I had to gain a certain number of hours working with people doing counselling, and so I went to work for the rape crisis centre near me. I found that not only did this help me to help others, but it also gave me the opportunity to help myself. Despite the many hours of understanding counselling I had received, something still seemed to be missing in my life, and by helping other people I came to 'find myself' more. I was able to put my own experience of suffering to good use by helping others and help myself heal at the same time. It was as if Spirit was always opening a new door once one closed, and I was being guided to the right people and right places.

All this was not to say that I always found my life easier. I had a great knowledge of Spirit now and of how we all live and pass over to this great world once we leave this one, but I still was living an earthly life with the pain and sometimes the suffering that we all have to carry. I found that my pain and suffering always had a meaning now though, and I could see that this life was like one big school and we were all here to learn all what we could while we were here and help our souls progress on in life. I found that my life was more advanced since this experience in the Spirit World, and I felt at times (and still do) that I wanted to run and shout and tell everyone all about the fact that this Earth isn't the only thing! We do live on, and we do progress and learn more in our earthly bodies and soul lives.

I did at times wish that I could go back to that place again and again throughout my life and experience what I had there, and not have to wait here on Earth until it was my time, but then I knew that what I had experienced wasn't just for me. It was so that everyone could see through my eyes what I had witnessed and know that this will happen to us all one day and is happening right now for those whom we have lost to the Spirit World. I want this knowledge to be passed on and on and talked about. I am just the vessel it happened to, and you are all the receivers of it.

Chapter Seventeen:
Physical Mediumship

M y energy with Spirit was becoming more and more profound. I was able to start training in what my mother and gran had done for years – 'physical mediumship'.

I always remember my mother telling me that when she was young she would go to large houses with my gran, and they would both work with Spirit in what is called 'materialization'. They would sit with a large group of people who would be called 'sitters', and they would be able to materialize spirits and objects from the Spirit World, while all of these people looked on in amazement. They would be called upon many times to do this, and every time without fail Spirit would come through them and give people comfort and messages from their personal loved ones.

Physical mediumship includes psychokinetic phenomena, such as the production of bangs and raps and the movement of objects with no seen cause. It also includes transfiguration, where the medium's face takes on the features of a spirit communicator, spirit voices which do not come through the voice box of the medium, and apports or objects that are materialized in the presence of the medium.

The hardest and more powerful part of physical mediumship is called 'materialization'. Materialization is the creation of matter from nowhere and out of nothing. The most famous example of a materialization comes from Christianity and is the story of the multiplication of bread and fish by Jesus to feed a hungry crowd. Usually, a materialization will be manifested on the form of ectoplasm; this is a semi-fluid substance that often appears cloudy and white. The word 'ectoplasm' comes from the Greek and literally means 'exteriorized substance'.

Ectoplasm can be manipulated into hardened rods, and Spirit can direct these rods to move large objects such as tables and chairs or to levitate a person. It can also be moulded into an artificial voice box or stretched out flat like a sheet of material with which Spirit cover themselves in order to lower their vibrations and become solid. In its primary stage it is invisible and intangible, but even then it can be photographed by infrared rays and weighed. In its secondary stage it becomes either vaporous or liquid or solid. In its final stages, when it can be seen and felt, it has the appearance of muslin and feels like a mass of cobwebs. At other times it is moist and cold, and on rare occasions dry and hard. Its temperature is usually around forty degrees Fahrenheit, which accounts for the observation of a drop of temperature around physical phenomena.

I asked my mother how materialization really worked and how it was possible, and she told me that there is a group of scientists in the afterlife who work with physical mediums to create communication between the dimensions. They use the energy of the medium and also the sitters who are watching to make the substance ectoplasm. They then use this ectoplasm and energy to make solid forms. They can use it to form themselves and the physical shape of when they were alive, or they can use it to form objects that may have meaning to the sitters. My mother said that it would need to be a dark room so that no lights could stop the ectoplasm from forming. To do this, it was sometimes best to use what they call a 'cabinet'. This is a dark box that will stop light from reaching the medium and where the sitters would be able to see the medium from the front of this cabinet. Ectoplasm is sensitive to light, so much so that even a flashing light drives the substance back into the medium with a strong force that can harm the medium! The medium has to work in the dark or in infrared light, and those responsible for their safety have to use absolute care in making sure the people watching can be trusted not to move and to stay still and hold hands.

My mother would tell me about the objects that had been given to her from Spirit. Once she told me that she was given a red rose from one of her loved ones. Everyone in the sitting could see this red rose, and some were able to feel it for a short time. She also told me about spirits that had formed in the room with all those watching (the sitters) and how solid they looked and how they had been the loved ones from the World of Spirit that had come back to try and communicate with a loved one in that room. I used to listen to this as a child and be amazed. I never understood fully what it meant, but I was always amazed to hear what had taken place for all those people watching.

My gran would tell me that when I grew up and was a lot older I would also be able to do this as Spirit wanted me to. She told me that it would take me years of training and meditation to perfect this, but with the love of Spirit and their help I would do this and be able to help many people.

Since my near-death experiences, the words of my gran are coming true. I was speaking to my mother about physical mediumship a few years ago, and this is when I knew that I had the gift to start training in this. It all started with my mother explaining it again to me, since I felt Spirit were guiding me down that path. I knew that the energy from Spirit around me could be used for good and be advanced to prove to people that there was a life after death. It was possible to see this with the naked eye, as well as hear a medium talk to you and say there was a loved one with you. It is human nature that we want to see things as well as hear them! And so this is why I wanted to develop physical mediumship.

My mother hadn't done this type of mediumship for a number of years, but she was willing to teach me and train me. I am a very impatient person, as anyone who knows me will tell you, and so it took me a lot of tears and saying I would give up before I started to get results.

It started one late October night in the year 2005. I was sitting with my mother and father in the living room, and we decided to meditate and see if there were any spirits that wanted to communicate with us that night. My mother told me to sit and let Spirit communicate through me by using my energy and allowing myself to go into a semi-conscious state. She had trained me well in how to meditate and let Spirit come through my energy and use it to communicate, but to do it for real was going to take time and effort. I had tried to do this on a number of occasions and felt nearly at the point where I could let Spirit come through me, but I had never been able to fully achieve this. I had been able to go into a deep trance-like state and give great messages to my family and friends, but I had never been able to let Spirit use my space and energy enough for them to build in me or send objects through me.

I sat for a while and tried to meditate and go deep into this spiritual state. I asked Spirit to come through me and use my energy to build and try and communicate with me and my mother and father. It seemed like hours before I started to feel a total calm wash over me, and I felt as if I were back in the Spirit World. I could hear the voice of my mother telling me to speak and asking me who it was I had with me. I could see my gran with me in the Spirit World, and it was as if she was hugging me and giving me one of her cuddles. I could hear her talking to my mother and telling her to give me a gift. It only seemed as though I was in this state for a short time, and then I felt myself return to the room.

My mother was crying as she tried to explain to me that I had taken on the face of my gran, and she had been talking to my mother and father and had told them to give me a red rose. They both had seen this rose as a solid object, and my gran's face was solid and perfect through the face of my own. My father was also shocked and said that he too saw the face of my gran; he had also seen the red rose and reached out to take it from a hand that wasn't my own. He had felt the rose just as if it were solid. When he tried to take it from this hand, it was then that I was brought back to my surroundings. I guess my gran had felt happy knowing that I was given this gift, and she felt that this was enough for me and my training until the next time.

What we had all experienced was the start of my physical mediumship. The hard training that it had taken me was now paying off, and I would be able to develop this more. I had experienced this feeling for a short time. I asked my mother how long it had lasted, and she told me it was a good thirty minutes. I was amazed, because it only felt like seconds to me. This again showed me that time in the Spirit World has no limits.

I was also able to perfect the voice of Spirit coming through to me and others. This is where a medium uses a strange object called a 'trumpet' for communication with Spirit. It is a conical-shaped object with holes at both ends. The trumpet is placed in the middle of the circle, and the Spirit World will use the same energy as for materialization and let it float and talk through it. This is something I have done on many occasions, and it works well. We have had many of our loved ones talk to us this way, and it is an amazing thing to see and hear.

I now keep training in this energy, and I know that I have an ability to work with people using my physical mediumship. I have had many experiences with my family using this gift, but I now feel that it is time to use it to help others and let their loved ones come through. I feel that it has taken me time to perfect this, and I have had the best training in the world – that is from my mother and grandmother and also Spirit themselves.

Chapter Eighteen:
Final Thoughts

I feel that life for me will never be the same after this experience. I may have been through a lot of pain for my age, but I feel that this was part of my life's purpose and meaning. I see a future for me that will be one of helping others with the gifts I have gained from my near-death experiences and through my traumas.

I know that I was given this time and experience with Spirit to grow as a person and in return help others grow and understand the purpose of this life. I see life in a different way now, and I view things in my life a lot more positively. I was not always able to deal with life at times because of my spiritual gifts, and I felt that this new opening did at times cause me to lead a lonely path. Friends would not always understand what I had been through, and if I dared talk about my experiences, I would have been called many names. I did at times wish to stay alone for that is the place I could find my true self and I felt I didn't have to explain myself to everyone I met. Over time this changed, and the more work I did, the more I was able to help people and the more I understood my life purpose.

Now I see my path a lot more clearly, and my work is growing and growing, thanks to the help of a dear friend in my life who helped me write my first book and who helped me deal with the negative side of things in my life. I now find myself doing more for others and learning that we are all so different and that we all have a part to play in the Great Universe.

Learning about cosmic ordering from my friend has given me a new aim in life and helped me think on a more positive level. I could see that it was teaching me that we all create our lives through the way we think, just as we do in the Spirit World, where we create the place we want to be when we pass over to Spirit. It showed me that I didn't just have to feel this love and happiness in the World of Spirit, but that I could feel it in my earthly body as well and gain a lot of things in life that I wanted and needed. It showed me how to think with a clear positive view and know that what I was thinking was creating my life and what would happen. It was through cosmic ordering that I found a happy path in my earthly life and was able to go on and work helping others through my writing skills and spiritual work.

On this positive path, I learnt how to deal with the negative people we can meet on our path in life. I learnt how to distance myself from them so that they were not draining my energy, for people that are causing us distress do so by draining our life-force energy with their negative energy. It is as if they are taking the battery out of our body and using it to fill their own! You will hear from many spiritual people who will tell you that when you are spiritually minded, it is easy to feel human pain more. A lot of them are very sensitive like me. They not only take on this pain of others and feel for them greatly, but they can also be so gentle and sensitive that others can easily feel this good energy and fear it and try and take it away.

An example of this is in my life and the work I do. If someone feels that what I say isn't what they believe, they go around and try and harm me by saying I am a 'nutter' or I am in need of help. This is their way of trying to deal with the fact that they feel like this themselves, because they don't understand something. I have learnt to deal with this in a positive way. I send that person love and light through my mind, and I smile to myself as I know that what they say about me is in fact what they feel about their own lives. When I get called a 'nutter', it is in fact their way of saying, 'I am a nutter because I can't get my head around what you are saying.'

You see, life is a mirror. We give out from this great mirror, and what we give is reflected back to ourselves. If we give out good, we get good back. If we give out bad, we are going to get bad back. This mirror is our thinking. If we live a life where we feel happy by running others down, we are going to get this back in our own lives because people will run us down. It is because we are saying to the Universe, 'I want this in my life!' So beware, because if you do give out bad vibes, you are asking for them back.

I hear so many people ask why they should be nice when everyone else is unkind to them. There is so much negativity that the world is like one big mirror giving more bad things back the more that are sent out, and so many people are getting hurt and feel that they have to look after number one. I did begin to feel this way, but I have learnt that I was in danger of attracting more negative people around me. Yes, it is also true that when we are kind to someone, we may not always get it back from them personally, but we will get it back another way because we have sent out into the Universe a message that says, 'I am giving out good, and I will get it back in my life.'

It is very much like the old saying that like attracts like – and that is also very true and the same as my universal mirror.

I can see the hardship in having to think this way when you have been hurt badly by life, but if you carry that hurt and let it rule you, then you are letting the people or person that has hurt you win.

Spirit speaks often to people about life and about our own personal journeys, and it is hard sometimes to follow a spiritual path with so much harm being done in the world. We have to know in our hearts that this isn't it! This isn't the truth and how it is meant to be. There is a more advanced reason for this life and its being, and we have to know in our hearts that we are here on this Earth to develop, be happy, and live a life that is rich for us and for who we are.

I had to change my thinking quickly when I left my trauma behind. I was living a life that was making me sad, and I was lost until I could see clearly that I had been through this for a reason and that reason was to help others and give to them a little of the knowledge that I had found from Spirit.

Spirit hadn't given this to me for myself. The knowledge had been given to me to show others that there is a special place that we all go to and that those we have lost are not gone. In fact, they are with you now as you read this! It is hard to take in and maybe believe to a degree, but what I was given and experienced was real and true. I tell you this, knowing that if I told you anything that was untrue, I would end up with that mirror coming back to me in ways I wouldn't like!

I see this world with new eyes now as well, and I see that there is at the moment a lot of war and trouble that rule the world and its people. I guess we all know about this and fear what is going to happen to the future.

Spirit speaks to me often, and I have given an insight about this Earth and about the trouble on it now. This trouble is like a point in life where there has to be change, and this change will come!

The war that man made will stop, and the pain that man is causing to the planet will stop, and the harm that is done to the people and creatures of this Earth will stop. No man can rule the Great Universe, for it is ruled by its own laws, and those are not the laws of man. Spirit has told me that change is soon, and the Universe is showing us this change already in what is happening to the planet itself. Many wise men and women have also heard of this change and also had Spirit tell them about it and its time.

This is not to scare you and make you think that the world will end! No, this is to show you that evil and negative people are not always going to keep taking over this Earth. Spirit and the Great White Spirit have seen all that is going on, and they see that the law of the Universe is out of balance and needs putting back to a balance. Spirit sees that good people are being persecuted for speaking out and evil is going on in the world that the simple man is not able to control. Spirit has told me that this balance will be back soon and will be for the good of all.

Over the past few years, many people have turned to the New Age way of thinking. People are seeking answers to this life, and more and more people are interested to know about Spirit and the afterlife. This is man's way of preparing minds and souls for the change that is taking place. It is Spirit's way of giving everyone a chance to see that no matter what goes on for the Earth and the evil that is being done, none of that matters, for they can't ever change the fact that this life is just the start!

Man can make war and create guns and bombs to kill and control. Man can think he has the upper hand if he has more money or more strength. Man can think he has won a fight if he sees another person weak and sick. Man can think, but thinking is all he is doing! For the reality is that this lifetime is for learning, and if that is all he or she has learnt and given to the planet, then you can guess that when they pass to the World of Spirit, they are the ones who will feel weak and lost and confused. They will see that all that effort in trying for power on Earth has gone now they are in Spirit, and the only power they have to learn is the power of that one word so many of us on this Earth have forgotten. That word is 'love'.

I hope that this book has given to you a journey that I myself took and that you yourself may take when you sleep or when you meditate. But I hope that above all you will feel the message and love that it is meant to bring you. Do not take my word for it alone. Listen to other people's experiences. Listen to your own experience as well, for that is the key to this book. You are special and unique, and no matter what you are told, always listen to your own little soul that is telling you what matters, for that is your personal journey.

I hope that I also one day will see you taking that 'walk on the other side' with me, and I would love in years and years to come to see the look on your faces when you meet with your loved ones and know that what I have told you is all so true!

Spirit be with you always!

X X X

About the Author

Charmaine Maeer was born into a spiritually minded family and was allowed to express her natural gifts of clairvoyance and healing from a young age. After many traumas in her lifetime, she now helps other people through her spiritual work in her home town of Dudley in the UK.

About the Book

Charmaine addresses something that comes to us all and to all our loved ones. It is something which we are very ill equipped to handle – death, the end of life, or the passing from one state, which we know, to another, which we cannot know.

A near-death experience – and the existence and reality of these experiences is well attested and undoubted – is a great and impressive glimpse behind the veil into another truer reality than that of everyday. Charmaine has the ability to communicate, and her writing is clear and lucid. She deals sensitively and perceptively with what can be a difficult subject. Behind her veil, is a brighter, vibrant, living truth. From her journey she has brought back much of value, a golden treasure, and she shares this.

Many of us would dearly wish to pierce, in however small a way, the veil that hides us from other worlds and to see what else is there. This book is one that helps us understand a little more the strange ways of creation.